THE PRIORITY OF MAKING DISCIPLES

THE MESSIAH AND OUR MISSION IN MATTHEW 28:16–20

Danny D. Clymer,
General Editor

First printing, August 2020

Master Books®, P.O. Box 726, Green Forest, AR 72638

Master Books® is a division of the New Leaf Publishing Group, Inc.

ISBN: 978-0-89221-766-3
Library of Congress Catalog Number: 2020939913

Cover by Diana Bogardus

Unless otherwise noted, Scripture is from New International Version NIV® Copyright © 1973, 1978, 1984 by International Bible Society®. Used by permission. All rights reserved worldwide.

Scripture quotations noted ESV are from the English Standard Version®, copyright © 2001 by Crossway, a publishing ministry of Good News Publishers. Used by permission. All rights reserved.

Scripture quotations noted Berean are from the Berean Study Bible, BSB. Copyright ©2016, 2018 by Bible Hub. Used by permission. All rights reserved worldwide.

Please consider requesting that a copy of this volume be purchased by your local library system.

Printed in the United States of America

Please visit our website for other great titles:
www.masterbooks.com

Master
Books®
A Division of New Leaf Publishing Group
www.masterbooks.com

CONTENTS

Foreword

In the late 20th century, a classic commercial suggested, "When E.F. Hutton talks, people listen." As disciples of Christ, we have known for centuries that when Jesus talks, *some* people listen. It is not only unbelievers who do not listen, but unfortunately, there are disciples of Jesus who do not always listen. Or maybe it is just a misunderstanding of what Jesus says. In Matthew 28:16–20 Jesus says to "make disciples," not just "be disciples." Of course, one must be a disciple to make disciples, but the latter seems to be the challenge.

This volume is offered to encourage disciple makers. Fourteen church leaders who have served in New England as disciple makers are the authors of these 12 sermons and the appendices. As you will see, each preacher has made disciples in the least churched and most secular part of the United States. Their commitment to hear Jesus, and their faithfulness to make disciples, are the reasons they are writing.

One goal for writing these sermons is to show the diversity of backgrounds of the preachers: small town, suburban, and urban; multicultural, black, and Caucasian. Jesus made no distinctions. He simply said to all disciples, "Make disciples." Another goal of this volume is to let the name of Jesus be most prominent. What the biblical text says is the title for each sermon. We want the true Author to be heard. The one exception is the last sermon, which serves as a summary for the entire text.

If funding allows, our hope is to give a copy of this publication to every preacher in New England. It is our prayer that some, if not all, of these sermons will be contextualized and proclaimed in each church and community. To be clear, this book of sermons is not another "how to" book. Its purpose is to draw attention back to the teachings of Jesus, whose mission was to seek and save the lost. Matthew 28:16–20 speaks for itself. It contains a focus on the Master and the message all disciples are to know in order to MAKE DISCIPLES.

— *Danny D. Clymer, Londonderry, NH*

1

Then

Matthew 28:16a

Jason McConnell \\ Franklin, VT

Introduction

No one in my family ever took me to church — not even on Christmas or Easter! My family didn't own a Bible, and I never heard any of the famous biblical stories like David and Goliath, Daniel in the lions' den, or even the death and Resurrection of Jesus Christ. I always thought Good Friday was good because it was a random day off school, and Easter was the happy spring holiday when I celebrated the hatching of Cadbury chocolate cream eggs.

I remember feeling embarrassed when Adam and Eve came up in conversation at my elementary school lunch table. I inadvertently revealed my religious ignorance when I asked, "Adam and Eve who?" My classmates looked at me like I was from another planet when they realized that I really didn't know who they were talking about. The only thing I knew about Christianity was what I had seen in horror movies. Crucifix-wielding priests, delivering the demonically possessed, gave me the impression that all religion was irrelevant — and weird. I honestly knew more about the devil than I did God.

By the time I was 16 years old, I was an angry agnostic alcoholic. I wasn't sure if I believed in God, but if he did exist, I resented Him. I didn't understand how a so-called loving God could let bad things happen to good people, or why He allowed me to experience so much tragedy in my young life. So, I pushed away the idea of a personal God and pursued a life of pleasure.

At the pinnacle of my impiety, my best friend and drinking buddy was involved in a horrendous drunk driving accident. He rolled his Jeep into a ravine; it flipped a dozen times before it hit a tree and stopped. By all accounts, he should have died, but he escaped with only a few minor bumps and bruises. When I saw him the next day, his face was still pale from shock. He said, "I think God spared my life!" I didn't argue with him.

As a result of this miraculous deliverance, he began attending a little country church just a few miles away from my house. I drove by the church every day, but I didn't know anything about it. A few months later, I heard a rumor that my friend had become a Christian and that he was now planning to become a pastor. I didn't believe it at first, but when I stopped by his house with a six-pack of beer one night, he confirmed the reports. He told me that he was "born again" and that God was "calling" him into the ministry. Then he invited me to come to church. I declined, but he was persistent. He eventually wore me down until I promised that I would go one time. The next Sunday, he picked me up and took me to his church.

Church wasn't at all what I was expecting! The people were not only normal, but they were warm and welcoming. I was amazed by the way they genuinely seemed to love each other. The pastor was young, and he preached in a way that I could understand the Bible's relevance to real life. As he preached about the perils of sin and humanity's desperate need for a Savior, I thought he was speaking directly to me. That day, I knew that I needed Jesus, but I wasn't ready to respond to the call of discipleship.

I was so impressed by the church, however, that I decided to go back the following week — and the week after that. Over the next few months, I got drunk every Saturday night, but I always got up in time to go to church on Sunday morning. Through the witness of my friend, the pastor, and the whole church, I began to see God for who He really was. The gospel of Jesus Christ became clear, and I finally heard the call of discipleship. On a cold Saturday night in February, I reached a high point in my discipleship journey; I finally professed faith in Jesus Christ and later was baptized.

When I woke up the next morning, I couldn't wait to tell my friend and the pastor what had happened to me the night before. As soon as church was over, I cornered them and recounted my story. They smiled at each other and said, "We knew it was just a matter of time before this happened to you." With confusion on my face, I asked, "How did you know this?" They said, "Ever since the very first day you walked into this church, everyone here has been praying for your soul! Welcome to the Kingdom of God!" I felt a cold chill run down my spine and my eyes welled up with tears. I had become a true disciple of Jesus Christ!

A Disciple-Making Church

As the weeks wore on, everyone in the church surrounded me with love and support, and my new faith began to grow. An older couple started hosting me for dinner after church every Sunday. They taught me how to read and understand the Bible. A small group of men taught me how to pray at the Wednesday evening prayer meeting. And I learned how to serve by watching worshipers of all ages use their spiritual gifts to help others in the church and community. I didn't know it at the time, but I had stumbled into a real deal disciple-making church. The church building was dilapidated and the sanctuary was disheveled, but the church embodied discipleship by mentoring people like me in every aspect of Christian life.

It was less than six months later that my pastor approached me and said, "Well, you've been walking with the Lord for a while now; it's probably time for you to preach your first sermon." Although I was intimidated by the prospect, I didn't know any better! I thought this must be a rite of passage for every new Christian at every church, so I answered, "Okay, but I don't know how to do it." During our weekly meetings, the pastor not only trained me in the fine arts of hermeneutics and homiletics, but he taught me how to live a holy life, how to evangelize my friends and family members, and how to think with a Christian worldview.

My first sermon went pretty well. The content was solid, but the delivery was lackluster. Even so, everyone in the church was encouraging and affirming. People began asking me if I had ever thought about becoming a pastor. I had never considered this before, but I began praying about it. A while later, when I preached my second sermon, I sensed the mysterious voice of the Holy Spirit saying to me, "This is what you are going to do for the rest of your life!" And sure enough, I have continued preaching since that day!

It wasn't until I moved away for college and began attending other churches that I realized how special this little country church was. The people in this church took discipleship seriously. They didn't buy into some pre-packaged evangelism program. They didn't outsource their discipleship to parachurch ministries. They didn't sell their souls to a newfangled church growth strategy. They didn't even sit around and talk about how to make disciples; they just did it! They simply believed Jesus' Great Commission and put its components into practice.

The Components of Discipleship (Matthew 28:16–20)

After Jesus rose from the dead and met up with the 11 disciples in Galilee, He took them up onto a mountain and delivered his now-famous Great Commission sermon. In Matthew 28:16–20, we read Jesus' words:

> Then the eleven disciples went to Galilee, to the mountain where Jesus had told them to go. When they saw him, they worshiped him; but some doubted. Then Jesus came to them and said, "All authority in heaven and on earth has been given to me. Therefore go and make disciples of all nations, baptizing them in the name of the Father and of the Son, and of the Holy Spirit, and teaching them to obey everything I have commanded you. And surely I am with you always, to the very end of the age."

There was nothing particularly complicated about this ministry model. Jesus wanted His disciples to believe that He was the King of heaven and earth. And since He had sovereign authority to reign over His whole Kingdom, it was His prerogative to use His disciples to expand His Kingdom. A knowledge of Jesus' divine authority gave His disciples the confidence they needed to proclaim the gospel and make more disciples.

The main component of the Great Commission is to "make disciples." This term literally means to bring someone into a teacher/pupil relationship. In this context, it means to bring people into a relationship with Jesus Christ, whereby they would learn Jesus' way of life and become His faithful followers. This imperative command dominates the passage.

Jesus directs His disciples to make more disciples with the threefold method of "going, baptizing, and teaching." The meaning of the term "going" has caused considerable debate among biblical scholars. Since Matthew uses the participial form, some have concluded that it has the force of "as you go" or "wherever you go." While the term certainly encompasses this sense, it also implies a deep compassion for lost souls and a deliberate effort to build relationships with sinners for the sake of the gospel.[1] Sometimes "going" may include something as simple as initiating a gospel conversation with a classmate or coworker, or it may be something as complicated as making a commitment to become a foreign missionary.

The next component of discipleship is "baptizing in the name of the Father, and of the Son, and of the Holy Spirit." When a person has understood the gospel in such a way that it produces repentance from sin and a true relationship with Jesus Christ, the believer will make a public profession of faith by being baptized in the name of the Father, Son, and Holy Spirit. Baptism (immersion under water) is the ordinance that outwardly identifies individuals with Jesus, and is a mark of true discipleship. The reference to the Father, the Son, and the Holy Spirit is given to

---

1. D.A. Carson, *Matthew, Expositors' Bible Commentary*, Vol. 8 (Grand Rapids, MI: Zondervan, 1984), 595.

distinguish an authentic Christian baptism from other types of baptisms. Jesus' statement about the three distinct persons of the Godhead would help the early church understand the nature of God and differentiate Christian orthodoxy from heresy.

"Teaching them to obey everything I have commanded you" is the final but ongoing component of discipleship. Disciples of Jesus Christ are called to teach Jesus' commands to other disciples. As a rabbi would take on a young pupil and convey the teachings of the Old Testament Law, a disciple will enter into an intentional relationship with another disciple and instruct him or her in all facets of the Christian life — everything from basic biblical truths to Jesus' specific teachings, to ministry skills that can be used in service to others.

The disciples at my little country church walked me through all of these components of discipleship. They listened to me and loved me for who I was. They met my physical needs while they ministered to my spiritual needs. They went out of their way to build a relationship with me for the sake of the gospel. They showed me my need for a Savior and introduced me to Jesus. They helped me repent from my sins, profess faith in Jesus Christ, and be baptized. One by one, they all taught me how to study the Scriptures, sacrifice and serve, pray and preach, and be a follower of Jesus Christ.

God used this little church of 50 or 60 people to disciple so well that many people heard God's call to become ministers in other parts of the world. Over a period of ten years, this little church sent ten people into full-time vocational ministry. I was number seven. Can you imagine that? A church that discipled people so well that it never grew in numbers.

This is one example of what a church can do when it takes the Great Commission seriously. Some churches get bogged down by elaborate strategies and complex programs. But true discipleship is really quite simple — Going, Baptizing, and Teaching. A church does not have to be large or even be located in a favorable demographic area to make disciples. The people just need to be willing to live out Jesus' Great Commission with authenticity, courage, and conviction.

The Call of Discipleship in the Gospel of Matthew

The Great Commission in Matthew 28:16–20 is the culmination of Jesus' call of discipleship. It contains a clear and concise formula for making disciples, but this process has already been displayed throughout Matthew's gospel. Matthew shows us many examples of how Jesus employed His own ministry method. It is interesting to view the Great Commission through the lens of Matthew's whole gospel.

Calling the First Disciples (Matthew 4:18–22)

In chapter 4, Matthew takes us back to the beginning of his public ministry. After Jesus was baptized and tempted by the devil, He launched His ministry in Capernaum, a town located along the banks of the Sea of Galilee. While He was walking along the beach, He encountered two brothers — Simon, called Peter, and his brother Andrew. Since these men were professional fishermen, it is no surprise to find them casting a net into the water. From the shore, Jesus yelled, "Come, follow me, and I will make you fishers of men" (ESV). A short time after this, Jesus came across James and John, the sons of Zebedee. They were cleaning their nets after a night of fishing. Jesus extended the same call of discipleship to them.

Notice how Jesus practiced the Great Commission before He ever preached it. He intentionally initiated discipleship with these two sets of brothers. He didn't sit back and wait for people to worship Him as the long-awaited Messiah. Instead, He applied the "make disciples" command to the going, baptizing, and teaching of the Great Commission. Although He already had a prior relationship with these men through their connection with John the Baptist (John 1:35–42), Jesus met these fishermen on their turf and connected with them on their level. He extended the call of discipleship in terms they understood. He would teach them how to "catch" men and bring them into the Kingdom of God.

In light of Matthew's whole gospel, I wonder if this text is trying to teach the Christian church that it is more important to practice the Great Commission than it is to preach it. It is certainly easier to talk about discipleship inside a comfortable church than it is to go and get our hands dirty by initiating relationships with the rough and rugged outside the church. Are we willing to establish relationships with people who are different from us for the sake of discipleship? How about our local churches?

Calling of Matthew (Matthew 9:9–13)

Later in the Gospel of Matthew, the author records his own call to discipleship. He was an improbable prospect to become a Jesus follower because he was a tax collector. As employees of the oppressive Roman government, tax collectors were considered sellouts by their own Jewish people, and they had a repugnant reputation for excessive extortion. As we see in Matthew 9:10, tax collectors were usually lumped into the same category as "sinners."

But as Jesus did with His first disciples, He went to Matthew and extended the simple invitation: "Follow me." And to everyone's shock and awe, Matthew left his lucrative career as a tax collector and became a follower of Jesus. He was so excited about his newfound faith that he invited his whole network of "tax collectors and sinners" to a dinner party in his home. He wanted all of his unseemly associates to meet Jesus and hear the same call to discipleship that he did.

Interestingly, when the Pharisees saw Jesus eating with people of ill repute, they asked His disciples why He ate with such uncouth characters. But Jesus overheard the question and responded with the clever quip, "It is not the healthy who need a doctor, but the sick. . . . For I have not come to call the righteous, but sinners." (Matthew 9:12–13).

Once again, we see Jesus applying His own Great Commission by "going" and "making disciples" among the people on the fringes of society. He was coordinating a cohort of unlikely candidates to form His inner circle of 12 disciples. As they traveled together, Jesus was teaching them to obey everything he commanded them (Matthew 28:20). Just in Matthew 9, we see Jesus teaching them about fasting (9:14–17), evangelism (9:35–38), and he showed them how to heal the sick (9:27–31), raise the dead (9:18–26), and drive out demonic spirits (9:32–34).

Once again, the Christian church can take its cue from Jesus' discipleship. As we go, will we associate with the unseemly in our society? Are we willing to compromise our clean reputations to "make disciples" among people of ill-repute? Do our hearts break for the broken and broken-hearted in our communities? Are we willing to follow Jesus' example by having dinner with a sinner for the sake of the gospel? Will we do our part to heal the sin-sick souls in our world today?

Sending Out the Twelve (Matthew 10)

By the time we get to Matthew 10, Jesus had assembled His full team of disciples. Their names are listed in Matthew 10:2–4: "These are the names of the twelve apostles: first, Simon (who is called Peter) and his brother Andrew; James son of Zebedee, and his brother John; Philip and Bartholomew; Thomas and Matthew the tax collector; James son of Alphaeus, and Thaddaeus; Simon the Zealot and Judas Iscariot, who betrayed him."

Certainly no one but Jesus would have seen such potential in four fishermen, a tax collector, a Zealot, and six "nobodies," but these are the 12 men whom Jesus called to be His disciples. They were neither wealthy nor famous; they were not particularly talented nor well educated. In fact, they were as average as could be. But Jesus employed His Great Commission model and called them to a life of discipleship. He personally invited each one, built intentional relationships with them, and taught them everything they needed to know about faith and life.

In Matthew 10:1, we see that Jesus "gave them authority to drive out impure spirits and to heal every disease and sickness." In Matthew 10:6–7, Jesus commanded them to, "Go . . . to the lost sheep of Israel. As you go, proclaim this message: 'The king-dom of heaven has come near.' " Notice how Jesus' words in Matthew 10 resemble His words in Matthew 28. This was the great commission before the Great Commission!

Every time I read this passage, I remember the words my pastor spoke to me when I was 17 years old, "Well, you've been walking with the Lord for a while now — it's probably time for you to preach your first sermon." I'm sure the Twelve didn't feel ready to drive out demons, heal the sick, or preach about the Kingdom of heaven, but Jesus empowered and unleashed them anyway. Why? Because this is discipleship! Jesus knew that they needed an opportunity to use their unrefined gifts for gospel ministry. The Twelve would make their fair share of ministry mistakes, but they would eventually go on to turn the world upside down.

Like the Twelve, I went on to make a lot of mistakes in my ministry, but at least the church gave me an opportunity, and they guided me along the path. It is amazing to contemplate the impact that a single church can have on a community (and maybe even the world) when it actually puts Jesus' Great Commission into practice!

Conclusion

As I continued to grow in my faith and received training (formally and informally) for ministry, God eventually called me to be the pastor of two small churches in rural Vermont. Over the years, I have tried to implement the same discipleship method that I learned from my little country church, which is simple obedience to Jesus' Great Commission. I am thankful that so many people in my current churches have caught the vision for meeting sinners on their own turf by building intentional relationships, speaking in terms that unbelievers understand, loving the unlovely, sharing the good news about Jesus' death and Resurrection, baptizing them in the name of the Father, Son, and Holy Spirit, and teaching them how to care for people's needs. They understand that by reading and understanding the Bible, fasting, praying, preaching, and evangelizing they will ultimately make more disciples!

Our churches haven't yet experienced the rushing waters of revival, but we have witnessed a steady stream of conversions and growth in the grace and knowledge of Jesus Christ! We have farmers and teachers and truck drivers and nurses and students who live out the Great Commission in our community every day. And over the last ten years or so, God has used our little churches in northwestern Vermont to send out missionaries, pastors, para-church workers, and marketplace ministers who are making disciples all over the world. Our churches have undergone periods of growth and decline, but we have tried to maintain our focus on building God's Kingdom rather than on growing our church. Our goal is to be obedient to Jesus' Great Commission and leave the results to God. We just want to keep proclaiming the gospel so that people hear the call to discipleship.

Addendum

During my first year of service as pastor of two small churches in rural Vermont, I encouraged the members of our fledgling youth group to invite some of their high school friends to a meeting. A few weeks later, the youth group almost doubled in size. Among the new students who came was a sophomore named Rebecca who immediately impressed me with her sharp intellect, quick wit, and good sense of humor. As Rebecca integrated into our youth ministry, she also began attending our church on Sunday mornings and the youth Bible study that my wife and I hosted at our home on Thursday evenings. Rebecca developed a heart for lost souls during our mission trips to Philadelphia and Montreal.

By her senior year, Rebecca was discipled to the point that she became one of the leaders of the Thursday evening youth Bible study. This role caused her to ask even deeper theological questions, and she expressed an intense desire to grow in her relationship with Jesus Christ. As a result of this, I invited Rebecca and two other students to join me in a small discipleship group where we would study theology and ministry skills at a higher level.

By the time Rebecca graduated high school, she was regularly using her spiritual gifts of leadership and evangelism to minister to people in our church and community. She went on to study Bible and philosophy at Wheaton College in Illinois. During college, she spent two summers doing youth hostel ministry in Europe and Russia. When she graduated from college, she sensed a call to full-time foreign missions. She has served as a missionary teacher at the Christian International School of Prague in the Czech Republic ever since. During the summer of 2017, my family and I had the opportunity to visit her and watch her thrive in her current ministry. It has been a joy and privilege to play a part in her discipleship journey!

2 The eleven disciples went to Galilee, to the mountain to which Jesus had told them to go

Matthew 28:16b

Michael Bailey \\ Bloomfield, CT

After His Resurrection, Jesus returned to Galilee where He met His first disciples — Peter and Andrew. The place where He bid them to come was the place of His final earthly command. But not all who had followed Jesus were there. His disciples went from thousands to 12 and now to 11. Judas, one of the 12, was absent.

A. Who Is Judas?

Judas Iscariot, the betrayer, is the one who sold Jesus for 30 pieces of silver and set the events that led to Jesus' crucifixion in motion. Judas ultimately hung himself because the priests refused to take back the "blood money" for which he sold Jesus.

> Then when Judas, his betrayer, saw that Jesus was condemned, he changed his mind and brought back the thirty pieces of silver to the chief priests and the elders, saying, "I have sinned by betraying innocent blood." They said, "What is that to us? See to it yourself." And throwing down the pieces of silver into the temple, he departed, and he went and hanged himself. But the chief priests, taking the pieces of silver, said, "It is not lawful to put them into the treasury, since it is blood money." So they took counsel and

bought with them the potter's field as a burial place for strangers. Therefore that field has been called the Field of Blood to this day. Then was fulfilled what had been spoken by the prophet Jeremiah, saying, "And they took the thirty pieces of silver, the price of him on whom a price had been set by some of the sons of Israel, and they gave them for the potter's field, as the Lord directed me" (Matthew 27:3–10; ESV).

Judas undoubtedly spent countless hours with Jesus and witnessed His work up close, yet he was lured by 30 pieces of silver. He exchanged his position in Jesus' "inner circle" for worldly desires. This is a reminder that one's physical location is no indication of where your heart lies. And as representatives of Jesus Christ, we must be mindful of how easily we can find ourselves in Judas' shoes. It seems as if many in this day and age are trading Jesus and the message of the Gospel for "silver" — the silver of power, fame, wealth, and popularity. Many of us are willing to sell our Christianity to the highest bidder.

As preachers, we have to take some responsibility for the dilution of the gospel. Too many of our messages have focused on God's blessings and not the person of Christ. The late 19th-century Presbyterian minister, Charles Finney, highlights this fact in one of his sermons saying:

> If there is a decay of conscience, the pulpit is responsible for it. If the public press lacks moral discernment, the pulpit is responsible for it. If the church is degenerate and worldly, the pulpit is responsible for it. If the world loses its interest in Christianity, the pulpit is responsible for it. If Satan rules in our halls of legislation, the pulpit is responsible for it. If our politics become so corrupt that the very foundations of our government are ready to fall away, the pulpit is responsible for it.[1]

---

1. Rev. Charles Finney, *The Decay of Conscience*, December 4, 1873, New York, NY, https://www.gospeltruth.net/1868_75Independent/731204_conscience.htm.

What Jesus came to do had no price. He couldn't simply write a check or swipe His debit card to pay for our sins. Instead, He had to sacrifice His life. And it is through the blood-bought work of Christ that our lives are truly transformed. When we fail to internalize this message, we are at risk to exhibit the same characteristics as Judas and exclude ourselves from God's promises. The consequence of forsaking Christ is eternal damnation, but there is an earthly penalty as well.

Our societal conscience depends on the gospel message because any foundation not rooted in Christ is in danger of collapse. But, if our confidence is in Christ, we can proudly share what the great hymnist, Edward Mote, wrote in verse 1 of "The Solid Rock."

> My hope is built on nothing less
> Than Jesus' blood and righteousness;
> I dare not trust the sweetest frame
> But wholly lean on Jesus' name.
> On Christ, the solid Rock, I stand;
> All other ground is sinking sand.[2]

In order for us to meet God face-to-face we must put our hope in Christ.

B. The Meeting at the Mountain of Galilee

Can you just imagine this meeting? Seeing the risen Savior? Many scholars have concluded that this mountain was the same one where Jesus was transfigured. He was transformed into a more glorious, radiant, and beautiful state, as told in Matthew's Gospel.

> And after six days Jesus took with him Peter and James, and John his brother, and led them up a high mountain by themselves. And he was transfigured before them, and his face shone like the sun, and his clothes became white as light. And behold, there appeared to them Moses and Elijah, talking with him. And Peter

---

2. Edward Mote, *The Solid Rock*, 1834.

said to Jesus, "Lord, it is good that we are here. If you wish, I will make three tents here, one for you and one for Moses and one for Elijah." He was still speaking when, behold, a bright cloud overshadowed them, and a voice from the cloud said, "This is my beloved Son, with whom I am well pleased; listen to him." When the disciples heard this, they fell on their faces and were terrified. But Jesus came and touched them, saying, "Rise, and have no fear." And when they lifted up their eyes, they saw no one but Jesus only. And as they were coming down the mountain, Jesus commanded them, "Tell no one the vision, until the Son of Man is raised from the dead" (Matthew 17:1–9; ESV).

It can be said that on this mountain the disciples were transformed themselves. No longer just watching Jesus' power at work, but commissioned to use that same power to do great works in His name. We can experience the same transformational power when we submit to Christ and dedicate ourselves to following Him.

I want to be a follower of Christ because it grants me access to the meeting where I can experience the love and glory of Christ. Knowing that Christ's love changes you and revolutionizes the world, don't you want to experience this wonderful state and place? This is why it's key that we regularly "meet" with Christ through prayer, fasting, and study.

C. We Need Jesus

Being a part of the gospel's journey makes a world of difference, as we have direction by way of the Holy Spirit. We see great demonstration of the Holy Spirit in the Book of Acts, particularly chapters 1–2, as Jesus ascends to heaven and leaves us His presence. The Greek and Hebrew words for "spirit" can also mean *wind* or *breath*. I like to think about the wind of the Lord blowing us, the breath of the Lord resuscitating us, and the Spirit of the Lord living on the inside of us, all important as the 11 prepare to go to the mountain (John 20:21–22; Acts 1:8).

Matthew 28:16b carries great significance. While we may become discouraged by the absence of Judas, who walked and talked with Jesus, much like the other disciples, we can celebrate the fact that the other 11 disciples obeyed Jesus at this time in God's history. It was not in Jerusalem that Jesus told them to go, but to a mountain in Galilee of all places. Their faith, with all of their misunderstandings about Jesus, led them to this mountain.

I was always taught in Sunday school that grace is the Lord's unlimited favor through the gospel, and we will never experience grace in its full propensity unless we obey Christ. I was also taught in Sunday school that mercy is the withholding of what I deserve, which is death and destruction because of my sin. And the sin of man is what separates us from Jesus Christ. This sounds very drastic, but it's real. Jesus came and fulfilled a plan of success in spite of the world's destiny of disaster. But it's through the gospel and God's great love that we are no longer separated, but reunited with Christ. The Apostle Paul says,

> Who shall separate us from the love of Christ? Shall tribulation, or distress, or persecution, or famine, or nakedness, or danger, or sword? As it is written,
>
> "For your sake we are being killed all the day long; we are regarded as sheep to be slaughtered."
>
> No, in all these things we are more than conquerors through him who loved us. For I am sure that neither death nor life, nor angels nor rulers, nor things present nor things to come, nor powers, nor height nor depth, nor anything else in all creation, will be able to separate us from the love of God in Christ Jesus our Lord (Romans 8:35–39; ESV).

This love is beautiful and so simple. It was Thursday that He ate His last supper. He went to the garden to pray but was arrested. He was tried and found guilty although He was innocent. But, it was His mission to die for the guilty so that we could stand before the throne innocent. They beat Him, ripped His clothes, and put a crown of thorns on His head. They nailed Him to the Cross. They gave Him vinegar when He was thirsty, and pierced Him in His side to ensure He was dead. While He hung on the Cross in agony, Jesus still showed love when He said, "Father, forgive them, for they know not what they do." He died so that we can experience the greatest love.

They thought they killed Him, but no man killed our Savior; He laid down His life willingly. It was love that got Him up Sunday morning. He told them that He had all power, and instructed His disciples to share the Word and to do great works with that power that came from the Resurrection.

And now the call is to us. We are to go and make more disciples, to extend the invitation to meet Christ. We may not be physically meeting at the Mountain of Galilee, but wherever we meet Him can be a place of transformation. When we bow our hearts to Jesus and proclaim that we want to follow Him, the scales fall from our eyes and all things become new. Then the cry of our hearts will be,

> I want to be a follower of Christ.
> I want to be one of His disciples.
> I want to walk in the newness of life,
> So let me be a follower of Christ.
>
> What do I have to do?
> What do I have to say?
> How do I have to walk each and every day?
> Tell me what does it cost, just to carry the cross?
> So let me be a follower of Christ.[3]

Addendum

Currently, I am discipling a few young men from different parts of the world who live in close proximity to me in Connecticut. I am intrigued by each of them and their stories. I like to believe

---

3. Joseph W. Harris, "I Want to be a Follower of Christ," 2008.

I am a positive voice in their lives, but I also realize they are impacting me all the more. One particular young man whom I have spent a great deal of time with is a former semi-professional football player.

He sought me out by way of his mother because he was in a downward spiral after the death of his sister. His sister was killed in a car accident, and he was burdened with a myriad of negative emotions as a result. But perhaps the most crippling was unforgiveness. He would often challenge me by questioning God's justice.

As of now, the person who was at the wheel of the car that fatally hit his sister is a free man. One could argue that he received a "slap on the wrist" by merely being sentenced to community service. It is natural to believe that in this particular situation, justice wasn't served. But instead, the driver was shown undeserved mercy by the judge. These situations can make you quite angry and hateful when you feel that justice has been withheld. Through our conversations, I have been encouraging him to discover the power of forgiveness and the nature of Christ. He has been teaching me that we do ourselves a disservice when we try to measure justice according to our earthly scale.

There is a great need for the gospel to spread throughout the world because it is a reminder that we all are guilty of sin, yet Christ has set us free. The blood-bought work of Christ allows each of us to be declared not guilty of crimes we surely did commit. When we recognize the grace and mercy that has been extended to us, we can more willingly extend forgiveness to others. Our relationship with Jesus Christ doesn't make it easy to forgive, but it makes it possible. Jesus allows us to trade the burden of unforgiveness for His yoke of freedom.

This young man recently accepted Christ as His Lord and Savior and was baptized. He has married his college sweetheart, and together they are expecting their first child. The work of the Lord is coming to fruition in this young man's life. Again, I must confess that I am learning more about the power of the love of

Jesus Christ and the presence of His Spirit through this particular young man — learning to love someone who has essentially impacted your life through tragedy.

3

When they saw Him, they worshiped Him

Matthew 28:17a

Frank Reynolds \\ Candia, NH

What do you think of when someone mentions the Great Commission? Many Christians immediately reflect on the words, "All authority in heaven and on earth has been given to me. Therefore go and make disciples of all nations. . . ." Certainly, some would think evangelism, missions, discipleship, or maybe the authority of Jesus. But I doubt they would think about worship.

What does worship have to do with the Great Commission? Well, maybe everything.

We are considering Matthew 28:16–20. We read in verse 16: ". . . the eleven disciples went to Galilee, to the mountain where Jesus had told them to go." Verse 17 reads, "When they saw him, they worshiped him; but some doubted." What do Jewish fishermen do when they worship? Do they visit the closest synagogue and sing Jewish songs, or do they dance?

In this message our focus will be three words: "they worshiped him."

The Backstory

This scene takes place somewhere in Galilee. Chapter 28 begins with the climax of Jesus' earthly journey — the Resurrection. The first 27 chapters of Matthew tell us about Jesus' birth, baptism, and temptations in the desert. There are five major teaching blocks, miracles, and the growing tension with the religious leaders which culminated during Jesus' final Passover. The following is what brings this tension to its boiling point:

- Only John tells us about the raising of Lazarus prior to the final week of Jesus' public ministry. The leaders now intend to kill both Jesus and Lazarus.
- Sunday is the Triumphal Entry. The tension grows.
- Monday is the day of authority where Jesus cleanses the temple. The tension is about to boil over.
- Tuesday is the day of controversy — a verbal boxing match between the religious leaders and Jesus.

The chief priests and elders throw the first punch asking, "By what authority are you doing these things? . . . And who gave you this authority?" Jesus blocks them with a question about John the Baptist: "John's baptism — where did it come from? Was it from heaven, or of human origin?"

> They discussed it among themselves and said, "If we say, 'From heaven,' he will ask, 'Then why didn't you believe him?' But if we say, 'Of human origin' — we are afraid of the people, for they all hold that John was a prophet."
> So they answered Jesus, "We don't know."
> Then he said, "Neither will I tell you by what authority I am doing these things" (Matthew 21:23–27).

Then Jesus throws three quick jabs — pow, pow, pow — three parables, each exposing the hypocrisy of the leaders. It was not a fair fight, but they keep trying until finally no one dared to ask him any more questions.

Jesus concludes this boxing match by sharing with the crowds in the temple courts seven woes aimed at the hypocrisy of the teachers of the law and the Pharisees. It is as if Jesus was pushing them, forcing them to devise a plan for His death, which He was, and which they did. He painted them as "whitewashed tombs, which look beautiful on the outside but on the inside are full of the bones of the dead and everything unclean" (Matthew 23:27).

Behind closed doors, "they schemed to arrest Jesus secretly and kill him. 'But not during the festival,' they said, 'or there may be a riot among the people' " (Matthew 26:4–5). Judas Iscariot solves their dilemma. He provided a time and location where they could arrest Jesus discreetly.

This leads us to the arrest, trials, beatings, and Crucifixion of Jesus. The great expectations of the Apostles are shattered. The One they had confessed to be the Messiah was now dead, in a tomb, and all was lost; or so they thought.

God Put the Need to Worship Inside Us

It seems everyone loves a good drama, whether in real life, a book, a movie, or their favorite sports team. I believe God put that in us. In New England we love our sports, sometimes in a twisted kind of way. We love to hate the Yankees. The Yankees losing is more important than the Red Sox winning, unless they are playing each other.

When Jesus died on the Cross, the ninth inning was over. The Apostles lost. All who believed Jesus was the promised Messiah lost; not just a league championship or a World Series, but everything. It was the greatest tragedy in the history of mankind.

But three days later, God took *the greatest tragedy in the history of mankind* and turned it into *the greatest victory for mankind*. The Resurrection changed everything! The Resurrection brings us to worship. But. . . .

First, we need to understand worship. We worship, or at least we think we do.

What Is Worship?

Before we get back to the Apostles in Galilee, we need to pause and think about how we worship. We can express worship in many different ways. But there is a deeper question. What is worship? We do not need to define worship in order to do it. In fact, we will worship whether we can define it or not. However, we cannot accurately evaluate our worship without an adequate definition.

I am going to use two passages to help us understand acceptable worship. For some of you, I will leave out your favorite verse or verses, but you are welcome to use your favorite passage to evaluate my definition. Here is what we are after: an all-encompassing sentence which defines acceptable worship before God. Here is my definition: Worship is a life-expression of praise and thanksgiving for who God is, what He has done, what He is doing, and what He will do.

Worship Must Be Our Whole Life

We tend to think of worship as an individual expression. Worship is expressed in many ways, but without the whole-life expression, all the individual expressions do not count. If you doubt what I am saying, carefully consider Isaiah chapter 1 where there are multiple unacceptable expressions of worship.

> Verses 11–12: Israel expressed their worship through sacrifices — not acceptable.
>
> Verse 13: Israel expressed their worship through offerings — not acceptable. Israel expressed their worship through incense — not acceptable. Israel expressed their worship through special assemblies — not acceptable.
>
> Verse 15: Israel expressed their worship through prayers — not acceptable.

How could these be unacceptable when God was the One who established these expressions of worship for the Israelites? They had turned acceptable expressions of worship into religious stuff which had nothing to do with their everyday waking, walking, talking, and living.

When I travel to Rwanda, it is the norm to be asked to preach each Sunday I am there. We arrive at the church service about 10 a.m. Some have been there since 8:30 a.m. They have been sing-ing and dancing for about one hour. Two or three choirs will sing multiple songs; more dancing. About 11 a.m., Theophile (my partner in Rwanda) will let me know it is time to preach. That takes another 45–60 minutes with an interpreter. When I am finished, another church leader will get up and review what I just preached. After a few more formalities, we are finished.

For some Rwandans, their expressions of worship are accept-able to God. Of course, that is for God to judge, not us. How-ever, the key point for us to understand is that not all the expres-sions of worship that Sunday morning may have been acceptable to God.

What about the man who loves to sing and dance in the Sunday service, but walks out the door and cheats on his wife? He abuses his children. He steals from his neighbor. He partic-ipates in corrupt business practices. Next Sunday he returns to the "worship" service because he loves to sing and dance. Is that acceptable worship? Of course not!

Our expressions of worship must flow from our whole lives. Then, and only then, are the multitude of worship expressions offered in a variety of cultures acceptable to God.

Worship Is Focused on God

Worship is about the One being worshiped. Worship is not about us. It is about Him. He is worthy. We are not. Paul says it this way:

> Therefore, I urge you, brothers and sisters, in view of God's mercy, to offer your bodies as a living sacri-fice, holy and pleasing to God — this is your true and proper worship" (Romans 12:1).

Based on the message the Apostle Paul has shared in chapters 1–8, there is only one reasonable response: God, here is my life, struggles and all, warts and all, hang-ups and all, temptations and all. This is all I have. This is me. In my brokenness, I offer my life to You as an expression of praise and thanksgiving for who You are, for what You have done, for what You are doing, and for what You have promised You will do. I acknowledge You are worthy.

In 2002, it seemed like the whole country, except California, was rooting for the New England Patriots to win their first Super Bowl. They beat the St. Louis Rams 20 to 17. We celebrated. Since that year, the Patriots have been in eight Super Bowls, winning five more. Some of the losses were heartbreakers. I still feel the sting of the 2007 Super Bowl loss to the Giants with the infamous helmet catch by David Tyree to snatch defeat from the jaws of victory. Eli Manning should have been sacked and never have had the opportunity to just sling the ball. I am not bitter or anything, just because a fluke play robbed us of a perfect 19-0 season.

Why focus on one game when there are so many sweet victories? How about the defensive Super Bowl in February 2019 against the Los Angeles Rams, or Super Bowl XLIX against the Seahawks when Malcolm Butler made a goal line interception leaving 20 seconds on the clock. People were jumping off the couch that night.

I think my favorite was Super Bowl LI against Atlanta on February 5, 2017. My wife, Myra, and I were in Spain visiting one of our granddaughters, Haizea. Her parents, Rebekah and Ruben, just happened to be there. In Bilbao, the game started at 12:30 in the morning. When the Falcons went ahead 28-3 with 8:31 left to play in the third quarter, the other three fans in Bilbao began falling asleep. I knew a comeback was possible, but not easy. Another six minutes and the Patriots scored their first touchdown of the game, but missed the extra point.

In the fourth quarter, 19 points behind, we witnessed a Hightower strip-sack, a Tom Brady 15-yard run, and an Edelman miracle catch. My dilemma was when to wake the others up. If I wake them up only to lose, I'm in trouble. If I don't wake them up and we win, I'm in trouble. Once we won the coin-toss in overtime, I woke them up to see one of the greatest come-backs in sports history. Four minutes into overtime James White crossed the goal-line to give New England their fifth Super Bowl victory, and Patriot fans all over the world were celebrating. It reminded me of the prophecy that old men will spin in their wheelchairs, old women will throw popcorn, young children will do cartwheels, and high-fives will be shared by my executives and servants, both men and women.

Yes, there was a great celebration. And there should be. God put that inside of us. Whether it is one of the top events in sports or peewee football, we enthusiastically celebrate a great play or an amazing win. But we should keep one thing in mind: it's only a game.

God is so much greater. Because of who He is, He is worthy of our praise in every season and from every generation.

> But you, LORD, sit enthroned forever; your re-nown endures through all generations (Psalm 102:12).

When I think about what God has done, I am reminded of cre-ation, Abraham, Isaac, Jacob, Joseph, Moses, the exodus, Joshua, the judges, the kings, the prophets, Daniel, the lion's den, a fiery furnace, Nehemiah, Esther, John the Baptist, Jesus, the Apos-tles, and so many more. Did we leave anyone out? Of course we did. Perhaps we will spend a portion of eternity just sharing how God's faithfulness in history has been demonstrated over and over. He is faithful! He is not just the God of the past. He is working in our lives today. He is working in my life today.

When I finished seminary, Myra and I left Lincoln, Illinois, with no debt, but no money. We weren't sure how we would make it back to Virginia, but we did. In June of 1980, just six months later, we had enough financial partners to move with our nine-month old son to Manchester, New Hampshire. Seven years later, we were able to drop all outside support. We believed God opened the door for us to work with the Manchester Christian Church. And so, in worship, we praised God for His provisions.

For 30 years (and six more children), God was continually faithful. Then in 2010–11 we believed God was opening a new door to equip leaders for the Church in Rwanda, Africa, and beyond. In worship, we took a step, and guess what? God was faithful to us then, and continues to be faithful to this day. We can trust Him to be faithful in the future.

1 John 3:1–3 says,

> See what great love the Father has lavished on us, that we should be called children of God! And that is what we are! The reason the world does not know us is that it did not know him. Dear friends, now we are children of God, and what we will be has not yet been made known. But we know that when Christ appears, we shall be like him, for we shall see him as he is. Everyone who has this hope in him purifies himself, just as he is pure.

This confidence always results in worship like that written in Revelation 4:11:

> "You are worthy, our Lord and God, to receive glory and honor and power, for you created all things, and by your will they were created and have their being."

"They Worshiped Him"

Let's return to Galilee. Recently, the odds had been worse than a 70-yard Hail Mary with a second left on the clock. And the stakes were much higher than any Super Bowl. The Apostles were willing to bet their lives on the One they believed to be the Messiah. But He had died on a Cross. Now, He's alive!? They had all seen the risen Lord previously. We just can't be certain how many times and how long these encounters lasted. "Then the eleven disciples went to Galilee, to the mountain where Jesus had told them to go. When they saw him, they worshiped him" (Matthew 28:16–17.

Matthew, who was there, uses a word for worship that means to kneel or prostrate oneself on the ground. Although there is some danger I will overstate the significance of the scene, let me tell you what I think is happening.

Discipleship Begins with Worship

Matthew uses the word "worship" 12 times. Here are a few examples:

- Magi from the east came to worship him (Matthew 2:2).
- On a high mountain, Satan offered Jesus all the kingdoms of this world if He would bow down and worship him. Jesus replied: "Worship the Lord your God, and serve him only" (Matthew 4:10).
- After Peter had walked on water and then doubted, Matthew tells us, "Then those who were in the boat worshiped him, saying, 'Truly you are the Son of God' " (Matthew 14:33).

The scene in Galilee is not the first time the Apostles worshiped, but something changed. For the 11, they have journeyed from "come and see" to "you are the Christ" to "let us make three tabernacles." But something changed. Now they are bowing before the risen Lord. Risen means He had died. All hope was gone! But now He is alive. Mourning has turned to exuberance. Despair has turned to joy. Is this even possible? But here He is, in our presence. And "When they saw him, they worshiped him" (Matthew 28:17).

After 3½ years they are all but ready for the Great Commission. They only need one more thing — the gift the Father promised, which happens on the day of Pentecost. But here in Galilee they receive their marching orders. They have now physically and spiritually bowed before the risen Lord.

Back in the nineties, during a small group study in Tom and Judy's home, there was a knock on the door. Cindy, the next-door neighbor, needed to borrow some sugar. She was invited to join our small group and was soon attending regularly. After a brief time, her husband Bill was attending. I would describe Bill as an agnostic with honest questions. As the journey progressed, Steve and I were invited to Bill and Cindy's home to answer some deeper questions. We knew the pivotal issue for Bill was the Resurrection — did Jesus rise from the dead? After some discussion and a few book recommendations, we left Bill with a few assignments. We had confidence he was competent to pursue his questions with a little direction.

After a short period of time, Bill and Cindy made the decision to follow Jesus with all their lives. Bill shared with the congregation, "I now believe Jesus rose from the dead. I don't know where this will lead in my life, but I am ready to follow."

Bill and Cindy made a decision to worship the risen Messiah with all their lives, to bow before Him in worship.

Is it possible to be a disciple of Jesus without worship? Well, perhaps, if you have a shallow view of discipleship and a shallow view of worship: raise-your-hand-if-you-want-to-go-to-heaven view of discipleship. But this view is impossible when we are dealing with the biblical view of discipleship and worship.

This is similar to the thoughts of Dallas Willard in his book, *Renovation of the Heart.*

> Those who are not genuinely convinced that the only real bargain in life is surrendering ourselves to Jesus and his cause, abandoning all that we love to him and for him, cannot learn the other lessons Jesus has to teach us. They cannot proceed to anything like total spiritual transformation. Not that he will not let us, but that we simply cannot succeed. If I tell you that you cannot drive an automobile unless you can see, I am not saying I will not let you, but that you cannot succeed even if I do.[1]

---

1. Dallas Willard, *Renovation of the Heart* (Colorado Springs, CO: NAV Press, 2002), p. 66.

Jesus said, "And whoever does not carry their cross and follow me cannot be my disciple" (Luke 14:27).

On a mountain in Galilee, the 11 have become that kind of disciple. They are ready for the Great Commission because, "When they saw Him, they worshiped Him."

What does worship have to do with the Great Commission? Well, maybe everything.

Addendum

Bill became convinced of the historicity of the Resurrection and decided to follow Jesus, wherever that led, whatever that meant. He was now a disciple, a student of Jesus. Bill had a coworker, friend, and golf buddy named Ted. Ted was divorced and was coming from a narcissistic past. But through Bill, Ted began attending Sunday services. Both men had a desire to grow spiritually. With one more friend, we began meeting weekly for breakfast. We studied New Testament letters, memorized Scripture, and reviewed books together (like *The Call* by Os Guinness). In confidence, we shared real life struggles of men, husbands, and followers of Jesus. Increasingly, these men, and their wives, applied themselves to ministry roles in the local church. It was a joy to witness the growth happening in them and their families. But this was not just about them and their growth. This was also about me and my discipleship. They were not my disciples. This was about four men being discipled by the Master Teacher. We were on a journey together, learning to worship and follow the risen Lord.

4

But some doubted

Matthew 28:17b

Tim Hawkins \\ Boston, MA

OOPS — Upset Equilibrium

Have you ever heard the advice, "If something seems too good to be true, then it is"? I'm sure you have but if not, you might want to write that down! It's an important part of doubting.

I do not have an official/written-down bucket list. If I did, watching the Boston Bruins play in a Game 7 Stanley Cup Final in person would certainly be on my list. So, when that rare opportunity became a reality this spring, I began to scour ticket sites to find the best deal. Everywhere I looked, the cheapest tickets were $1,200, $1,500, $2,000, except for one site where the tickets were $350! My antenna immediately went up: "If something seems too good to be true, then it probably is!" It is not surprising that the very next day there were postings all over the Internet warning people to be wary of scam ticket sites selling "very cheap tickets." I'm glad I didn't pull the trigger! I'm guessing you can relate. Maybe it wasn't Bruins tickets, but it was that vacation package where you could go three nights and four days for almost free, or that car you have been looking for that was advertised much lower than anywhere else, or maybe it was that profile picture that caught your attention, only to not recognize them in person! But what happens when doubt and suspicion become the way we see the world?

Peter David, who is best known for his comic book work and the writing of *Star Trek*, recently wrote a novel called *Tigerheart*. In it he describes the growing suspicion in the world around us. "When you are a child, there is joy. There is laughter. And most of all, there is trust. Trust in your fellows. When you are an adult . . . then comes suspicion."[1] Operating as an adult is to know when to hold some things in suspicion. But what happens when we begin to hold everything in suspicion? When we no longer know what is true? When experts are cited for both sides of every argument? When nothing seems absolutely true?

I. UGH — Analyze the Discrepancy

In this series we have been looking at the text from Matthew 28:16–20:

> Then the eleven disciples went to Galilee, to the mountain where Jesus had told them to go. When they saw him, they worshiped him; but some doubted. Then Jesus came to them and said, "All authority in heaven and on earth has been given to me. Therefore go and make disciples of all nations, baptizing them in the name of the Father and of the Son and of the Holy Spirit, and teaching them to obey everything I have commanded you. And surely I am with you always, to the very end of the age.

We are going to spend our time on only three words: *but some doubted.*

If this were a social-media post, I might think Matthew was throwing shade at some of the other disciples on the mountain that day! You can imagine all the disciples engaging in small talk as they made their way to Galilee and up the mountain. A few expressed some hesitation about why they were even going to the mountain, and then Matthew passively-aggressively throws someone under the bus — ". . . but some doubted (eyes emoji)."

---

1. Peter David, *Tigerheart* (Los Angeles, CA: Del Ray, 2008), p. 216.

Jesus was performing miracles, confronting religious hypocrites, and spending time with the down and out. Jesus was, in many ways, too good to be true, offering freedom and salvation and everlasting life. It is not surprising that large crowds began to follow Jesus. It's also not surprising that many found Jesus too good to be true. Of the hundreds (or thousands) of people who were beginning to follow Jesus, Jesus chose these 12: Peter, Andrew, James, John, Philip, Bartholomew, Matthew, Thomas, James, Simon, Judas, and Judas (there was a serious lack of creative names in the 1st century!) to be His inner circle. Eleven of the 12 make it to this story — make it up the mountain. These are Jesus' closest followers, those He chose to disciple. In fact, Matthew would tell us that Jesus spent an entire night praying to decide who His first disciples would be. And these were salt-of-the-earth people. People who survived with a healthy amount of skepticism.

I wish faith came easy for me. It does not. It takes a while for me to trust anything, especially people. Maybe it comes from living in Somerville, MA/New England for almost 15 years.

I remember my first week in Somerville. I accidentally parked my car in front of my neighbor's drive, and he knocked on my door at 9:00 a.m. to let me know. You would have thought I had committed a capital crime. He shouted, "I don't know how people park in Missouri, but around here people don't park in front of their neighbor's driveway." (Of course, I'm leaving out many adjectives he placed in between!) I don't think he talked to me again for 2 years. I eventually moved deeper into the middle of Somerville. I have lived on my current street for 12 years, and it took 10 years for my neighbor, Sal, to finally wave at me. Now I need to avoid Sal unless I have at least 30 minutes to chat! We don't trust people easily in New England — that is something I have learned through experience. Doubt serves us well. It helps us discern if something is too good to be true, if people are too good to be true . . . if they can be trusted. It took 10 years of not parking in front of Sal's driveway for him to finally trust me, and I do not take his trust lightly! Trust/faith is not simply about information — it is about the source, about who shares the information. We'll come back to this in a bit.

II. AHA — Clue to Resolution

The 1st century language used to preserve these stories and then to write them down is known as common Greek. It is the language of everyday people, like you and me. And when Matthew uses the Greek word *distazo*, which translates into English as "doubt," it is the second time Matthew uses it in reference to at least one of the Apostles. The other time is found in Matthew 12. We pick up the story right after Jesus feeds a huge crowd of thousands with only five loaves of bread and two fish. If you saw this with your own eyes, it would certainly make you a believer, or would it?

> Immediately Jesus made the disciples get into the boat and go on ahead of him to the other side, while he dismissed the crowd. After he had dismissed them, he went up on a mountainside by himself to pray. Later that night, he was there alone, and the boat was already a considerable distance from land, buffeted by the waves because the wind was against it.
>
> Shortly before dawn, Jesus went out to them, walking on the lake. When the disciples saw him walking on the lake, they were terrified. "It's a ghost," they said, and cried out in fear.
>
> But Jesus immediately said to them: "Take courage! It is I. Don't be afraid."
>
> "Lord, if it's you," Peter replied, "tell me to come to you on the water."
>
> "Come," he said.
>
> Then Peter got down out of the boat, walked on the water and came toward Jesus. But when he saw the wind, he was afraid and, beginning to sink, cried out, "Lord, save me!"

Immediately Jesus reached out his hand and caught him. "You of little faith," he said, "why did you doubt?"

And when they climbed into the boat, the wind died down. Then those who were in the boat worshiped him, saying, "Truly you are the Son of God" (Matthew 14:22–33).

We already live by faith that some things matter — some things are worth doing and believing in. But doubt is never far from the picture. And when we doubt, faith is never far from the picture. We do not live out of doubt. We do not jump out of the boat and walk on water from doubt. We do not love from doubt. We do not hope from doubt. Faith got Peter out of the boat. Faith took the disciples to the mountain. This is how Peter, and how I, can go from walking on water to sinking in a matter of steps.

Our great doubt is not so much in the existence of God (most of us believe in the existence of some higher power), *but we doubt whether or not God is good.* This is not a doubt of evidence, research, or reason. It is a relational doubt. If God is good, then things in the world, in my life, should be different. Linda should not have died of cancer, Justin should not have died of a stroke and left two small boys behind, and Tyler should not have had a debilitating stroke at the age of 35. These are all close friends of mine that I have watched go through these hardships in the past few months. I suspect you have your list, too. And I think Peter had his list. "Is God good?" is my great doubt.

III. WHEE — Present the Good News

I was in the third year of college ministry, working at a college with a big aviation program, when I was asked to speak at a church that is by very definition "in the middle of nowhere." It was four hours away — a miserable distance! Many of those I worked with were aviation students, and when mentioning the trip to one of them, he said that he would be glad to have an opportunity to log the flight hours if I would buy the fuel. While I was excited at the prospect of saving eight hours of driving time, my fear of flying was worse than my dread of the drive. I know the research shows that driving is statistically more dangerous than flying. I know that the laws of nature and physics make flying reasonable. And I know that the evidence suggests, despite logic, that the 747-8, which has a maximum take-off capacity of nearly 1,000,000 lbs., *can* fly from LA to Melbourne, Australia.[2] I get it. But I don't FEEL it! So, when I got into the four-seat Cessna, I did so partially because I had done some homework, seen the data, and read about the physics. I mostly boarded the plane because of Matt. I trusted that Matt would pilot my flight safely. Other students had asked me to fly with them, but I had not done so. However, I trusted Matt. He had proven to be thorough, trustworthy, conscientious, thoughtful, humble, and detail oriented. I'm not sure any of these qualities are prerequisites for admission to flight school, but they earned my trust!

When the disciples met Jesus at the mountain, they brought their list of doubts, yet they came with faith in the person of Jesus. This could mean that some of the 11 doubted, while the others worshiped. If this is the case, I can certainly relate. Like Peter, I have had the same sense of faith and doubt within what seems like only a few steps. It's not the doubts and questions that move us forward. It is faith that always helps us take the first step. And faith is relational: Whom do we trust?

I want to suggest something to you. Faith and doubt are not in opposition; they are in constant companionship. They are, in fact, in a perpetual dance — a dance that keeps us from buying Bruins tickets from a nefarious website. But it is a dance that gave me the courage to ask my wife on a date — even though I doubted she would say yes. I didn't ask blindly, but there was plenty of doubt! As someone who struggles with a healthy dose of doubt, I have found this explanation of the dance between faith and doubt helpful. It is a quote from an author named Lesslie Newbigin. In his book, *Proper Confidence: Faith, Doubt & Certainty*, he says:

---

2. https://en.wikipedia.org/wiki/Boeing_747-8

One does not learn anything except by believing something, and — conversely — if one doubts everything one learns nothing. On the other hand, believing everything uncritically is the road to disaster. The faculty of doubt is essential. But as I have argued, rational doubt always rests on faith and not vice versa. The relationship between the two cannot be reversed.[3]

What Newbigin is saying is that everything we do is already built on faith. We already live our lives with some faith in the ideas that love matters, faith that our actions matter, faith that hope matters, faith that justice matters, faith that we can know anything at all.

Jesus personally steps into the problem of pain and suffering. Jesus weeps over death. Jesus gets angry with greed corrupting the systems of the world. Jesus Himself experienced betrayal from loved ones and endured the pain of crucifixion. Listen to Jesus' words as He suffered on the Cross: "About three in the afternoon Jesus cried out in a loud voice, 'Eloi, Eloi, lama sabachthani?' [which means 'My God, my God, why have you forsaken me?']" (Matthew 27:46). Jesus understands our doubt in the darkest moments. What took the 11 to the mountain was not hope in another dreamer who died for a lost cause, but belief that the person of Jesus was raised from the grave. The Resurrection of Jesus meant that pain and suffering would be swallowed up, that war and hatred would come to an end, that justice and mercy would become the way of life. It meant that life could come through the worst of circumstances. This is the Good News: in Jesus we have the hope of life in the worst of circumstances.

In his book *Faith and Doubt*, John Ortberg tells a story about a friend named Cheryl who has multiple-sclerosis and went to a salon for a manicure. As the stylist began working, they enjoyed good conversation about a number of things until the topic of God came up. "I don't believe God exists," the stylist told Cheryl.

Cheryl asked, "Why do you say that?"

---

3. Lesslie Newbigin, *Proper Confidence: Faith, Doubt & Certainty in Christian Discipleship* (Grand Rapids, MI: Eerdmans, 1995), p. 25.

The stylist responded by pointing out all the suffering in the world, sick people, abandoned children. She concluded, "I can't imagine loving a God who could allow all these things." Cheryl did not want to start an argument, so she let the conversation be. The stylist finished her work, and Cheryl left the shop. Cheryl saw a woman in the street with long, stringy, dirty hair. Cheryl walked back into the shop and said, "Beauticians do not exist."

The stylist replied, "How can you say that? I am here. I just worked on you. I exist!"

"No," Cheryl explained, "beauticians do not exist because if they did, there would be no people with dirty, unkempt hair like that woman outside."

The stylist responded, "Ah, but beauticians do exist. The problem is, people do not come to me."[4]

We can all acknowledge things are not right in the world, and we can even admit that we do not always do things the way we should. We are not always as kind, loving, forgiving, or generous as we want to be. On our most honest days, we can even acknowledge that we sometimes contribute to the ugliness in the world. Circumstances may have you doubting whether or not God is great. However, those same circumstances outside of your control may also cause you to throw up your hands and cry out to God because there is no other name, no other hope, no other possibility that can pull it all together. There is no other power by which those same circumstances might be able to bring about some good. That is why the story doesn't end at Jesus' death, but with ongoing Resurrection that has the power to bring life from death. Serena, a Suffolk doctoral candidate in Psychology said it well to me over coffee recently, "I think I only feel God in a relational way when I am desperate." That is when doubts don't matter.

IV. YEAH — Anticipate Implications

There are many who are not certain about Jesus. But Jesus did not ask for certainty, only faith. And that, smaller than a mustard

---

4. John Ortberg, *Faith and Doubt* (Grand Rapids, MI: Zondervan, 2008), p. 117–118.

seed. Think about this for a minute. My guess is you don't think you have enough faith. But Jesus said this, "Truly I tell you, if you have faith as small as a mustard seed, you can say to this mountain, 'Move from here to there,' and it will move. Nothing will be impossible for you" (Matthew 17:20). A mustard seed is very, very small. Yet, with faith that small, you can move a mountain. I don't think I've ever moved a mountain, not a real one anyway. But, if it only takes that much faith to move one, how little faith did it take for the Apostles to climb the mountain to where Jesus was after the Resurrection? How much faith does it take for you to reach out to God when there are no other options? Doesn't that make God the best option? Doubt is a given, but doubt isn't fuel! It can never take you anywhere.

I want to suggest to you that your doubts are not strong enough to keep you from following Jesus. Jesus may be too good to be true, but He is worth taking a step of faith toward. Religion is not. Please do not confuse the two. I'm not suggesting that religion is worth your faith. It isn't. Most of us don't believe in religion anymore. We don't believe in the institution. Fortunately, Jesus did not say that the institution is the way, the truth and the life. Jesus said that He was. Faith is relational.

Jesus' closest followers had just enough faith to make it to the mountain that day. They worshiped *and* they doubted. That is all it takes for you and me to take that step of faith today with our faith and doubts. I want to suggest three things for you if you are struggling with doubt:

1. No one does it alone. Faith is something we do together. The Apostles climbed the mountain and worshiped and doubted together. Faith is not an individual activity, it is a relational and communal way of life.

2. Confess your faith (what you believe in) as well as your doubts. Because you will find that what you believe in aligns closer to Jesus than trying to live with faith in nothing.

3. Let go of the idea that you need to be perfect. Faith does
    not mean perfection. It only takes a mustard seed, and
    God hears our faith within our most desperate moments.

All you need is just enough faith to take the first step. Others
will stand beside you with their faith and their doubts. At that
moment, you either put your faith in nothing and sink beneath
the pounding waves, or muster just enough faith to reach out
and believe that God can make something good from this. Even
though my doubts say Jesus may be too good to be true, it only
takes a mustard seed of faith to find life again.

Addendum

Yisu came to college with doubts and questions. Yisu was a proclaimed atheist throughout high school, but the loss of a friend
began to trigger deep questions for her about her faith in atheism. In his book *Soul Cravings*, Erwin McManus suggests there
are three deep-seated testimonies about God at work in our lives:

1. Our desire for intimacy
2. Our desire for destiny
3. Our desire for meaning[5]

Yusi began to wrestle internally with whether or not her atheism
could fulfill her desire for destiny and meaning. This happens in
the heart and life of every human being. The question we want to
ask in discipleship is, "Where will people turn and to whom will
they turn to answer and process these questions as they search for
meaning?"

A phrase I repeatedly use with my campus ministry team is,
"Ask God to give you a front row seat as a witness to the work
God is doing in people's lives." The other thing I am sure they tire
of hearing me say is, "You want to love people so well that you are
the first person they think to call in a moment of crisis." Discipleship begins way before someone goes public with their questions.

---

5. Erwin McManus, *Soul Cravings* (Nashville, TN: Thomas Nelson, 2006), table of
contents.

In our ministry, we talk about these students as spiritual wanderers. When Jesus says, "Therefore, as you go…" it is because the harvest is plentiful, but the workers are few. In fact, the fields are ready for the harvest and as you go, making disciples is the key.

In 2018 Pew Research showed that America's trust in church/organized religion fell below 40% for the first time since they began tracking the statistic in 1973. In fact, trust has fallen by 10% from 48%-38% in just the past five years.[6] And this is especially so among young adults. In 2019, Pew updated their findings saying, "Faith in expertise and institutions has declined, cynicism has risen and citizens are becoming their own information curators."[7] What has become more and more valuable are the people we trust. In 2017, the American Press Institute released a study that showed, "When Americans encounter news on social media, how much they trust the content is determined less by who creates the news than by who shares it, according to a new experimental study from the Media Insight Project, a collaboration between the American Press Institute and The Associated Press-NORC Center for Public Affairs Research."[8]

What does this have to do with discipleship and Yisu? It took her some time to warm up to our community on campus at Northeastern University, but ultimately what she encountered in that small group of students were honest, open, loving, inquisitive people looking for truth and sharing the truth they had found in Jesus.

6. https://www.pewforum.org/2018/06/13/young-adults-around-the-world-are-less-religious-by-several-measures/.

7. https://www.pewresearch.org/2019/06/05/an-update-on-our-research-into-trust-facts-and-democracy/.

8. https://www.americanpressinstitute.org/publications/reports/survey-research/trust-social-media/

5

All authority in heaven and on earth has been given to me

Matthew 28:18

David Smith \\ Nashua, NH

Introduction

What is the first word that comes to mind when you hear the word "ministry"? I imagine for some of you, it is the word *discouragement*. If you are not battling it now, you have, and you will. Discouragement chases those in ministry, especially those in leadership.

The great English preacher Charles Spurgeon, no stranger to discouragement, said this: "Usually cheerful as we may be, we must at intervals be cast down. The strong are not always vigorous, the wise not always ready, the brave not always courageous, and the joyful not always happy."[1]

In Scripture, we see God's leaders fighting discouragement. Despite a great victory over the prophets of Baal, the threats of Jezebel send the prophet Elijah spiraling into discouragement. "I have had enough, LORD. . . . Take my life; I am no better than my ancestors" (1 Kings 19:4).

I. Why Do We Become Discouraged?

We are human: Spurgeon again, "When at last a long cherished desire has been fulfilled, when God has been glorified greatly by our means, and a great triumph has been achieved, then we are apt to faint. It might be imagined that amid special favors

---

1. Charles Spurgeon, *Lectures to My Students* (London: Passmore and Alabaster Press, 1897), p. 186.

our soul would soar to heights of ecstasy, and rejoice with joy unspeakable, but it is generally the reverse. Poor human nature cannot bear such strains as heavenly triumphs bring to it. There must come a reaction. Joy and excitement are often followed by discouragement."[2] Are you feeling your poor human nature?

We feel God has let us down: Elijah to God, "I have been very zealous for the LORD God Almighty. The Israelites have rejected your covenant, torn down your altars, and put your prophets to death with the sword. I am the only one left, and now they are trying to kill me too" (1 Kings 19:10). Is your life what you expected or desired? Is your ministry of making disciples what you imagined?

We experience rejection: We feel alone, unwanted, forsaken by God and others. "I am the only one left, and now they are trying to kill me too."

We take our eyes off God: Like Elijah, we listen to the words of others and forget the Word of God. Overwhelmed by the present, we fail to remember the presence, the power, the promise of our God who says, "All authority in heaven and on earth has been given to me" (Matthew 28:18).

Remember the authority of Jesus: When you feel discouraged with your ministry, when you wonder what or why or how you can make disciples, remember the authority of Jesus. **Remember the authority of Jesus.** Biblically, to remember is more than to look backwards. It is to bring a past truth into your present reality. If we are going to overcome our discouragement, and persevere in making disciples of Jesus Christ, we need to **remember the authority of Jesus.**

II. As We Go

He rules: All authority in heaven and earth has been given to Jesus. With His Resurrection, the arenas in which Jesus now exercises His authority include heaven and earth — the universe. This authority has been given Him by the Father, so the Father

---

2. Helmut Thielicke, Translated by J.W. Doberstein, *Encounters with Spurgeon* (London: Lutterworth Press,1963), p. 130.

is exempt from His Son's authority. His Son becomes the One through whom God exercises His authority.

God vindicates Jesus for His humiliation at the Cross. As Paul reminds us, the One who calls us to make disciples, the One who commands us to go, is in very nature, God. But this Jesus did not consider equality with God something to be hung on to at all costs.

> Rather, he made himself nothing by taking the very nature of a servant, being made in human like- ness. And being found in appearance as a man, he humbled himself by becoming obedient to death — even death on a cross! Therefore God exalted him to the highest place and gave him the name that is above every name, that at the name of Jesus every knee should bow, in heaven and on earth and under the earth, and every tongue acknowledge that Jesus Christ is Lord, to the glory of God the Father (Philippians 2:7–11).

Our Lord has all authority. "All" dominates the verses in Mat- thew 28:18–20 and ties them together: all authority, all nations, all things (everything), all the days (always). Jesus has all author- ity. His authority is no longer limited, as it was when He walked the earth, limited not in power, but in reach. As those called to lead God's church, we need to remember that wherever we go, everything is subject to the authority of Jesus. What an encour- agement! This Jesus who is with us always, this Jesus who will never leave us nor forsake us, has all authority.

Every morning I think on these words from Psalm 46:10: "Be still and know that I am God." This verse reminds me that God is God, and I am not. There is great freedom when we embrace this truth. God wants us to be still, to cease striving, and rest in Him. *He rules.* He has all authority. He has given it all to Jesus. As you seek to make disciples, are you resting in the authority of Jesus? Who leads your church or ministry? You, or Jesus through you?

Jesus is Lord. He reigns. One day every knee will bow before Him and confess His Lordship. He is King. He is worthy of worship. Making disciples matters because worship of Jesus matters. *Remember the authority of Jesus. He rules. He commands.*

He commands: The authority of Jesus should encourage us. There is nothing we will ever encounter outside His authority. But this authority means He has the right to command. He commands and we obey.

Therefore, because Jesus has all authority, we and those we lead are to make disciples as we go. Our ministry is universal — all nations, in Jerusalem, Judea, Samaria, and to the ends of the earth. Universal authority leads to universal mission.

Question: If everything is under His authority, then why is ministry so discouraging? Why are people so difficult? Why is life so challenging? Perhaps you have asked these questions. I know I have.

Here is an illustration. When God called us back to New England a second time, I was excited to return to Crossway Christian Church, the church I helped plant back in October 1995. I left Crossway in August of 2000, to return to my home church and oversee their church planting ministry. Over the next 16 years, I served in both church and parachurch roles, most of them connected to church planting.

One day in January 2016, I received a call from the man who followed me as Crossway's lead pastor. He asked if I would pray about returning to Crossway to plant a campus in the downtown part of our city. After praying about it, God made it clear He wanted us to do it. We returned to Nashua, New Hampshire, two months later.

I had great visions of what we would do as a downtown campus. As people expressed interest, I emphasized again and again our vision of seeing God work through us to transform our city. I was not interested in just being a place for people to go worship. I wanted us to be a church for our city. I wanted us to be the church, God's people, in our city. I wanted God to work through us to transform the lives of lost and hurting people.

There were challenges from the start. The building we bought fell down, making us front page news for three days, but thankfully, killing no one. There were delays related to insurance payments, materials, construction, inspections. We did not begin public worship until a full two years after I had returned. But the delays gave us extra time to build relationships in the community, as well as a brand-new building.

In many ways, things are going well. We are growing, people are coming to faith, believers are reaching into the community, some are growing in maturity. But not like I envisioned. Not like I pray. Where is the authority of Jesus? Where is the power of Acts? Honestly, it feels more like I am serving God's church in the time of the Old Testament prophets, calling God's people to return, to pray, to serve, to give, to know this Jesus, become like Him, and do the things He does. And yet the response has been underwhelming. Where is the authority of Jesus?

As I have wrestled with this, I have been reminded that Jesus, in His authority, restrains His authority. Whether you believe God's grace is resistible or irresistible, He restrains His authority. Either way, we don't know who will respond and persevere. It can be so discouraging to work with people whose hearts reflect the first three soils in Jesus' parable of the soils. Who doesn't want to work with the fourth soil? Yet Jesus, in His authority, does not make everyone produce fruit 30, 60, or 100 times.

So what do we do? As we go, we make disciples. We persevere in leading God's church, trusting in Jesus in whom resides all authority in heaven and on earth.

We go because *He rules, He commands, He calls us to make disciples.*

He calls to ministry: I remember when God called me into ministry. When I was a new believer, I participated in something called a lay witness mission where a team of lay people go into a church for a weekend to share their faith, listen to others' stories, lead small groups, worship, and pray with the hope of seeing God bring renewal and revival. My first mission was at the Milton United Methodist Church in Milton, Kentucky, just across the Ohio River from Indiana. I went with my wife, Nancy, and her parents, who had participated in a number of these missions.

It was a Spirit-filled weekend. We saw God move as lost people came to faith in Jesus, and found people committed to live more fully for Him. There was a moment when I was by myself that I experienced Jesus in a way that has not been repeated. I was shaving and heard footsteps on the carpet in my bedroom. When I looked out of the bathroom, I saw no one visible. The presence of Jesus, however, was overwhelming. I literally felt it. On our way home, I sensed God calling me into vocational ministry. I knew if it was real, it would last, as I had two and a half years left on my Army commitment. It did, and here I am today more than 36 years after that weekend.

Still, there are times I want to walk away from it. I get tired of ministry, and I imagine you do too. We wonder what it would be like to do something different. We dream of something easier, something more measurable. We identify with Elijah and all those who know the discouragement of ministry. Why don't I just leave and do something else? But I remember the authority of Jesus. This authority is not only a comfort, but a calling to obey. Jesus called me into ministry. This is what I will do until He calls me to do something else. *Remember the authority of Jesus. He calls us to ministry. He calls us to place.*

He calls to place: I don't know how you landed at the church you serve. Perhaps you sensed a direct call from God Himself. You identify with Paul who, upon seeing the vision of the man from Macedonia, left at once, concluding that God had called him to preach the gospel there. Maybe you sense more a general call to ministry and feel the freedom to go where you want. You may be like those who say, "I don't know about being called, I just know I am sent."

Wherever you land on call to place, know this: you are where you are by the authority of Jesus. We make disciples because of the authority of Jesus, whether we go across the street or around the world. It is why we go. *He rules. He commands. He calls.*

The Greek word for authority is *exousia*. It occurs 102 times in the New Testament and means "the right to command or the power to act." The authority of Jesus is for the specific purpose of making disciples. It is why we do it. All this authority is resident in Jesus for the purpose of rescuing the world. This is all the authority we need to make disciples, and making disciples is what Jesus has called us to do. *Remember the authority of Jesus. It is why we go. His authority goes with us.*

III. His Authority Goes with Us

What an amazing truth! When we make disciples, the authority of Jesus goes with us. How?

It goes before us: Long before we ever touch people or place, God is working. Jesus says the Father draws, the Spirit convicts, and He builds. By the time we arrive, the authority of God Himself has already been working.

When our family first arrived in Nashua, New Hampshire, in 1995 to plant Crossway Christian Church, we knew no one. But God had already been working. He was already drawing people to be part of our launch team. He was already piercing the hearts of the unchurched with their need for God. Sometimes the authority of Jesus showed up in funny ways.

Upon our arrival, I joined the Chamber of Commerce. At the first after-work get-together, I won a drawing. It got my name, and our church name, out in front of many business people in our city. The next month, I was at a chamber gathering again, and just as they were about to have the drawing for the grand prize, I began to tingle all over. I turned to the person standing next to me and said, "I think I am going to win." Sure enough, they pulled my business card out and read my name and the name of our church again. I won a skydiving trip. The flustered chamber director, who did not understand why a church had joined the chamber, declared, "Well, I guess you'll be closer to God."

The next month I got a call telling me I had won a grand prize through a contest I knew nothing about. I thought it was a joke, so I never called back. They kept calling me, so I finally returned their call. It turns out my wife had written my name down and dropped it in a box at a hardware store. The contest was sponsored by a local newspaper, so once again my name, and the name of Crossway Christian Church, along with my picture, went all over town.

My staff joked that with my winning streak we needed to take our opening day offering and head to Las Vegas. We didn't, and I have not won a contest since. But the authority of Jesus that went before us continued to show up in miraculous ways.

We mailed out 60,000 postcards before we launched, at four different times. Still, my partnership team was skeptical about how many people would show for the first Sunday. They tried to talk me into launching with one service, instead of two, but I refused. I believed God was calling us to launch with two. Our first Sunday, over 500 people showed up! It was electric. I managed to preach them down to about 200 over the next ten weeks, but it gave us a great place for God to begin transforming this crowd into a church.

The authority of Jesus goes before us. God had already been at work in the hearts of people long before I showed up. I experienced the same authority working ahead of me when I returned years later to launch the downtown campus. This time it is through the favor God has shown us in the community, specifically with city kids, the homeless and under-resourced, and immigrants.

For example, we partner with a city organization that is not Christian. They have wonderful people who love kids and want the best for them. We help them with Thanksgiving, Christmas, and summer events, as well as helping kids after school with homework. They encourage their kids to come to our Kids Club, where every Thursday evening we serve food, fun, and Jesus.

Recently, we worked together to send 15 city kids to camp. Four of them were the sons of Rohingya refugees, a persecuted Muslim group. Again, the authority of Jesus went before us to open doors and hearts. The authority of Jesus goes before us. It also goes in us.

It goes in us: The authority of Jesus is more than a summons to obey. It is a power in us, as we make disciples and lead others to do the same. It is the power of God Himself.

When God first called me to New England to plant Crossway Christian Church, I remember thinking, "What do I have to offer? What do I know?" The answer was, and is, "Not much." But I obeyed both times and came with the authority of Jesus.

What is this authority? It is the power of God Himself. We see it displayed in Jesus in the gospels. Jesus demonstrates authority over disease, demons, nature, and even death. He demonstrates authority to teach, judge, and forgive. There is nothing outside the authority of Jesus. Jesus has all authority over spiritual forces, physical objects, industry, business, finance, media, education, science, families, neighborhoods, churches — everything and everyone.

This authority goes with us, not only in the God who goes before us, but in the God who lives in us, by the Holy Spirit. When we turn to the Book of Acts, we see this authority working in and through the lives of believers like us.

We see it in the words of Peter who denied even knowing Jesus. But when the risen Jesus ascends to the Father, and gives those early disciples the gift of the Holy Spirit, we see the authority of Jesus. Listen to Peter's Spirit-empowered words. "Therefore let all Israel be assured of this: God has made this Jesus, whom you crucified, both Lord and Messiah" (Acts 2:36). Again, "Silver or gold I do not have, but what I do have I give you. In the name of Jesus Christ of Nazareth, walk." (Acts 3:6). And again, "It is by the name of Jesus Christ of Nazareth, whom you crucified but whom God raised from the dead, that this man stands before you healed" (Acts 4:10).

The very authority of Jesus is with us as well. Remember His authority. Pray that Jesus Himself would empower your very words and deeds. The Book of Acts is Jesus continuing His authoritative ministry, by the Holy Spirit, through those first disciples. He wants to continue the story today. He wants to work in us. Remember His authority. *Do you believe in the authority of Jesus?*

Sometimes people ask, "How is ministry different now than it was in your earlier years?" In my earlier years, I would have said making disciples depends on God, but I still would have believed too much in my power to change the human heart. Decades later, I now know more than ever that the authority of Jesus changes hearts, that this authority is core to making disciples. It is God's work. He simply chooses to use us.

Don't give up. It is a privilege, as well as a responsibility, to lead with the authority of Jesus. God is always at work. He is doing things we can't see. He is moving upstream and underground. *Remember the authority of Jesus. It goes with us: before us, in us, after us.*

It goes after us: A few years ago, before I returned to Crossway for a second time, I was serving with my home church for the third time. (My oldest daughter accuses me of going back to churches I have previously served for encores and reunion tours.) I went with our senior pastor to Nairobi, Kenya, to see our partnership with Missions of Hope International. When we went to their school, Mary Kamau, one of the founders and directors, showed me the special needs room. She told me that one of the people from Crossway Christian Church had spent a month there so kids with special needs could learn about Jesus.

It overwhelmed me. When I prayed for Crossway after I left, I did not imagine the authority of Jesus showing up like this. A couple days later, we drove out to the high school where students come to live and be discipled for four years. As we approached the site, Mary showed me a gathering place, asking, "Do you see the roof? Someone from Crossway came for a short-term mission trip. When they saw we had no roof, they gave $100,000 so we could build a roof." I wept. I could not believe how the authority of Jesus reached out through Crossway so much farther than I had imagined.

Don't give up in making disciples. Don't walk away from those God has called you to lead. Remember the authority of Jesus. He is doing things you cannot see. He is doing things you cannot imagine. And when you leave some day, know that the gospel seeds you planted will bear fruit as God continues to exercise His authority long after you leave not only your church, but this very earth.

Addendum

I remember the first time I met Jim Kumorek. He came to Crossway Christian Church on Oct 15, 1995, our very first Sunday. When I asked him later why he came back, I was hoping to hear him say, "Your sermon was amazing!" Instead, he told me he was fascinated by the electric drum set. The drum set!

Jim grew up in a household where his mother was Catholic and his father did not attend church. By the time he was in high school, his experiences in the Catholic Church, and with his father, led him to doubt the existence of God.

At 23, Jim married Donna, a Catholic woman who attended Mass faithfully. He did not go with her. Neither one of them had ever heard, or at least understood, the gospel.

Over the next two years, Donna became spiritually disillusioned. She could not get pregnant despite infertility treatments. Weekly Mass was becoming less meaningful. The church only reached out when they wanted money. Still, Donna was hesitant to try something different because of her Catholic family. She also did not want to attend a church where everyone already knew each other.

In the fall of 1995, they began receiving the invite cards about the launch of Crossway. They threw away the first two but by the third one, they began to take interest. Jim told his wife if she wanted to try it, he would go with her.

That first year Jim and Donna continued to attend regularly, and he began to develop a relationship with our staff and volunteers. We allowed Jim to serve, as a non-Christian, in our tech booth. We wanted him to have a reason to come back, to hear the message of Christ, to see how disciples loved one another. Jim questioned freely, and we answered his questions.

After reviewing the gospel over a period of months with our staff, Jim confessed that he was a sinner who needed Jesus as his

Savior and was baptized. He began to grow exponentially. Jim was already a great servant before he was a Christian. You should have seen him after the Holy Spirit got a hold of him!

After I left Crossway the first time, Jim sensed God calling him to vocational ministry. One day we talked. He had accepted a position at a church in Peoria, Illinois. But some people were saying things like, "Why would you want to leave beautiful New Hampshire for Peoria, Illinois?"

And then Jim said this. "I thought following Jesus meant He was in charge, that He is Lord, and I do what He says." Wow! Talk about remembering the authority of Jesus.

6

Therefore go

Matthew 28:19a

Rick Francis \\ Scarborough, ME

These words of Jesus to His disciples, gathered on that mountain in Galilee, have been known through the ages as the Great Commission, and they have sparked missionary movements all over the world. For centuries, the focus of the Great Commission has been the spreading of the Gospel and the establishment of indigenous churches, with new disciples added to the Kingdom of God. The Scriptures have been translated into nearly every known language, and tools for teaching all that Jesus commanded have never been more abundant!

But just what did Jesus intend for His disciples when He told them to "go and *make* disciples"? Translators have differed in their understanding of *Go*. Some see it as an active command to get up and get going to the nations.

This has fueled great missionary zeal and has resulted in substantial movements in foreign countries. Others, however, see the grammatical construction (a participle) as saying, "as you are going," implying the need to make disciples wherever you find yourself. It is this latter understanding upon which this sermon is based.

However, over the past 50 years or so, the understanding of the term "disciples" has gotten a bit muddied. The church, particularly in the West, has shifted its focus from disciple-making to church growth, with success being measured in numbers of attendees and the size of the budget. Yet, after some relatively brief successes, the modern church overall has suffered decline, especially among younger generations. In New England, for example, the number of evangelicals is less than five percent of the population, with the majority of churches having significantly older memberships.

In many of the newer churches experiencing numerical growth, making disciples has become synonymous with some form of content-driven educational experience over a period of a few weeks. Once this is accomplished, the "disciple" is placed into service in the church alongside other team members with the hopeful expectation that everything will just work out for the best. Needless to say, this hasn't been very effective.

Somewhere around the 1980s, churches began following the business practice of developing mission statements. Some of these were quite impressive. They sounded biblical and seemed achievable. But very few sounded like the mission Jesus gave to His disciples in the Great Commission, simply to *Go and make disciples. . . .* Instead, we've so overcomplicated it that we've forgotten the importance of such a mission. And, sadly, we seem to have lost the definition of a true biblical disciple.

Let's look at three aspects of discipleship that can help bring us back to the true mission of the Christian Church.

First — What is a true disciple?

Why is this such a priority? Because the evidence of a healthy, thriving church is seen in the disciples it produces. Michael Breen of 3DM Movements says, "If you make disciples, you will always get the church. But, if you try to build the church, you will rarely get disciples."[1]

There's some debate in churches about how to define a disciple. The temptation is to define it as a job description. It may sound like this. A disciple is one who:

---

1. http://www.vergenetwork.org/2011/09/14/mike-breen-why-the-missional-movement-will-fail/.

1. Attends church and Sunday school regularly
2. Attends a discipleship class
3. Reads the Bible every day
4. Memorizes Scripture
5. Attends prayer meeting
6. Tithes to the church
7. Lives a somewhat sanctified life

The problem with this "task approach" is that these duties are evaluated by outward observation and can be easily duplicated by almost anyone. They are activities that unregenerate "Christians" can perform without ever having a living, personal, experiential relationship with Jesus. I've been in churches where some of the most unspiritual people appear to do pretty well with these outward behaviors.

So, what is a true disciple? If we're commanded and commissioned to go and make them in every nation, we need to know what they are.

And for their part, they all became *literal* followers of Jesus. They lived, ate, traveled, and worked with Jesus — learning what it meant to be true disciples.

But we also know not all His followers stayed true. In John 6:66 we read, "Many of his disciples turned back and no longer followed him," when Jesus' teaching challenged their own motives for following. When their interest waned, it was proof they were simply *fans* — not true disciples!

Second — How does a true disciple follow?

What was the difference between the 11 who stayed loyal and the rest who abandoned Jesus? Answering this question will help us discover the essence of the Great Commission.

I believe the answer can be found in John 15, where Jesus illustrates true discipleship with "The True Vine" narrative.

> "I am the true vine, and my Father is the gardener.
> He cuts off every branch in me that bears no fruit,

while every branch that does bear fruit he prunes so that it will be more fruitful. You are already clean because of the word I have spoken to you. Remain in me, as I also remain in you. No branch can bear fruit by itself; it must remain in the vine. Neither can you bear fruit unless you remain in me.

"I am the vine; you are the branches. If you remain in me and I in you, you will bear much fruit; apart from me you can do nothing. If you do not remain in me, you are like a branch that is thrown away and withers; such branches are picked up, thrown into the fire and burned. If you remain in me and my words remain in you, ask whatever you wish, and it will be done for you. This is to my Father's glory, that you bear much fruit, showing yourselves to be my disciples" (John 15:1–8).

It's helpful to visualize this illustration as much as possible. Jesus walked with His disciples for over three years. They'd been all over Israel and seen Jesus use objects from nature to make His teachings clearer. They'd seen the birds of the air and the flowers in the field. They witnessed miracles done to fig trees and watched money being drawn from the mouth of a fish. No doubt they had seen many vineyards dotting the countryside, as is still the case today. So Jesus uses a common species of grape to illustrate His teaching.

He identifies Himself as the Vine. His disciples are the branches growing out from the Vine, and they're expected to bear fruit. If they don't, the Gardener — God the Father — will break them off and use them to kindle His fire. And the branches that bear fruit can expect periodic pruning to become even more bountiful.

So why does Jesus use this as an illustration for disciple-making? Let's dig a bit deeper.

In the illustration, the vine is likely a grapevine which, as mentioned before, is very common in Israel. The vine itself is the source of life for the plant. With its root system, it provides the essential nutrients from the soil, conducts moisture, and springs forth with its leafy branches and abundant grapes. A grapevine of almost any variety is hard to kill. It keeps coming back no matter how hard you try to cut it down! It's fitting that Jesus would call Himself the Vine.

Again, Jesus labels His disciples the branches. The healthy branch comes *from* the vine and is kept alive and functional *by* the vine. A branch *detached* from the vine is a dead branch and will not produce fruit. But the branch that *does* produce fruit in Jesus' illustration brings forth lots of grapes.

Jesus further explains in verse five: "I am the vine, you are the branches. If you remain in me and I in you, you will bear much fruit; apart from me you can do nothing."

This brings us to the reason for Jesus relating the vine and the branches to making disciples.

The job of the branch is to bear the fruit the vine exists to produce!

Earlier, we looked at the traditional portrait often used to describe a disciple — mostly outward, performance-driven tasks. And we said, these are all learned behaviors that can be performed by most good students, whether or not they're true disciples. But if we assume for a moment they *are* true believers, what fruit is Jesus describing in His illustration that real disciples will produce? What fruit does Jesus, the Vine, expect to come forth from His branches?

Often, we label the good deeds people do as fruit. In many biblical contexts, this is entirely valid. After all, didn't Paul describe fruit this way in Philippians 4:17? In complimenting their generosity in his earlier time of need he writes, "Not that I desire your gifts; what I desire is that more be credited to your account."

Although good works can be called fruit, I don't believe that's what is illustrated by the grapes in this context. So, if not good works, then what? And how does this relate to disciple-making?

Most likely, the fruit Jesus was referring to in His illustration was an abundance of grapes — maybe something like the spies brought back from Canaan to show Moses. If so, these grapes each possessed seeds, and when they ripened and fell to the ground, they reproduced. That's what the disciples listening to this illustration would have gotten from it: an abundance of fruit with the capacity to reproduce. Could the grapes be the symbol for new disciples in this illustration? This is how the movement continues — Disciples abiding in the Vine and reproducing themselves.

Fast forward to the year 1875. By means of a genetic mutation, and some clever science, William Thompson perfected something different. By grafting cuttings from a Persian grape variety to existing rootstocks, he was able to produce seedless grapes! Today, nearly everyone has heard of Thompson's seedless grapes. They are the most popular grape in the United States. Yes, they are tasty and juicy, but they don't reproduce. But honestly, don't we all prefer seedless grapes?

When we focus on the fruit, we can often make it better, at least when it comes to food. But does it work with disciple-making? Did Jesus tell us to put our efforts into cultivating fruit or to abiding in the Vine? Jesus told His disciples to abide in the Vine and the fruit would take care of itself!

Over the past several decades, the church's focus has shifted almost completely from the *Vine* to the *fruit*. In fact, we may often forget about the Vine altogether.

The essential element to bringing forth much fruit is found in verse five: "If you remains in me and I in you, you will bear much fruit; apart from me you can do nothing" (John 15:5).

The source and power for fruit-bearing is Jesus. The key word here is *remains* (or sometimes translated *abides* — meaning to remain or live in). It describes a dependent relationship that recognizes its uselessness without the source of life.

To *remain or abide* in Him means to draw the essence of life from Him — the Vine. As 21st-century Christians, we struggle with understanding this. We confuse abiding in Him with activities like filling the seats on Sunday or attending a Christian concert. *Remaining* or *abiding* in the Vine is a difficult concept for many of us to grasp.

To *remain* or *abide* means to *forsake all idols*. This has been consistent with God's character forever, yet we still have our golden calves that cause Jesus to stay in the shadows of our lives.

To *remain* or *abide* is to make our home in Jesus as He makes His home in us! John gives us the seven *I am's*, each illustrating how this is what we need as disciples: the Bread of Life (6:48); the Light of the World (8:12); the Gate (10:9); the Good Shepherd (10:11); the Way, Truth and Life (14:6); the Vine (15:1); and the Resurrection (11:25). Each of these illustrates some unique characteristic of Jesus that's essential for our growth as a disciple. As we abide in Him, He lets His power flow from the vine to the branches and fruit, and more disciples — much fruit — is the result.

I think Paul understood this best as he spoke before the Areopagus in Athens in Acts 17:26–28 and following:

> From one man he made all the nations, that they should inhabit the whole earth; and he marked out their appointed times in history and the boundaries of their lands. God did this so that they would seek him and perhaps reach out for him and find him, though he is not far from any one of us. "For in Him we live and move and have our being."

That's *remaining* or *abiding* . . . to live and move and have our being in Christ. I can't think of a better description.

Personally, I struggle with consistently *remaining* or *abiding* in Him. As I mentioned previously, in ministry, the temptation is to focus on the fruit rather than the Vine. We want to be productive and show off *our* fruit, and again, we may be wrongly seeing fruit as our good works rather than as ourselves reproducing. But Jesus is clear — a true follower knows what it means to *remain* or *abide* in Him. After all, what kind of fruit can a branch create if it's not attached to the vine?

The consequence for non-abiding disciples is dire. Look at John 15:6:

> If you do not remain in me, you are like a branch that is thrown away and withers; such branches are picked up, thrown into the fire and burned.

In other words, spiritual firewood!

So, we've defined a true disciple and how a disciple follows Jesus and reproduces. Now comes the important question.

Third – What is getting in the way of true disciple-making?

Why are we not seeing an abundance of new disciples in our churches today? Could it be that the present disciples are not abiding in Christ and, therefore, are not reproducing? Are we spending too much time cultivating the seedless grapes (e.g., our programs and desires to build bigger and better ministries) rather than allowing Christ to work through us to grow, mature, and eventually reproduce according to His will for us? Are we more concerned about making spiritual firewood than true disciples? We need to stop focusing on what we call *fruit* and focus on Jesus, the true Vine.

I wish I could give you a list of things to do to be a better disciple. I'm afraid it's not what you *do* first, but *who* you *are* first. If you are connected to the right root you will produce the right fruit. And much of it. And it will have seeds so it *can* reproduce.

Since Jesus rose from the grave and ascended to heaven, living with Jesus has become a spiritual issue that must engage your very soul. He says that if you abide in Him and Him in you, implying that He will always do His part, then we *will* reproduce.

So, what should be our part? Look at John 15:7–10:

> If you remain in me and *my words remain in you*, ask whatever you wish, and it will be done for you. This is to my Father's glory, that *you bear much fruit, showing yourselves to be my disciples*. As the Father has loved me, so have I loved you. Now remain in my love. If you *keep my commands*, you will remain in my love, just as I have kept my Father's commands and remain in his love (emphasis added).

We are brought right back to the Holy Scriptures — making us wise unto salvation and as the standard for faith and conduct. In them we hear Jesus speaking to us. They inform our prayers and keep us connected to the Vine. They restore our souls when we are weak and laden with trials.

This is what the disciples in Jesus' day understood. It's also what the church fathers understood, and those who have kept Christianity thriving ever since: fruitful branches connected to the gracious, loving, life-giving Vine — our Lord and Savior, Jesus Christ.

Every follower of Christ needs to be about making disciples — as we go, wherever we go, being the seed God has called us to be. We must become true, Spirit-filled followers of Jesus Christ, abiding in Him, who make disciples as we go each day.

If we return to the simple mission Jesus gave through the Great Commission, *as you go make disciples of all the nations,* and we realize the power to accomplish this mission comes only from Jesus, the Vine, in "For in him we live and move and have our being" (Acts 17:28), we will once again see an abundance of disciples.

Addendum

Discipling done best is highly relational. Jesus' model of living with His disciples demonstrates the effectiveness of His life-on-life strategy as seen in the spread of the Gospel in the first century. The challenge in our culture is to replicate the relational aspects of Jesus' model and attempt to give adequate time to the development of other disciples. Tristan had been my student at the Bible College. He approached me with the request to be discipled and asked if I'd be willing to take him on. The answer was a quick "Yes!" We met together every two to three weeks in the beginning, where I learned more about his past and what brought him from Georgia to Maine. As an African-American young man, that was risky for him.

We bonded quickly and soon became good friends. He was curious about how to grow as a Christian, how to develop solid biblical relationships, and how to discern God's will for every aspect of future life. We shared our struggles and hardships and how God's faithfulness is unending. Before long we were brainstorming areas of ministry he might consider. He eventually became the youth minister at the church I was leading at the time. Later he got married and had children and served in social services as a career. We still meet on occasion and discuss how God is molding and shaping him and his young family. Time invested in this type of activity — disciple-making — is never wasted. Tristan now has his own disciples and is applying what he's learned in his role as disciple-maker!

7 Make disciples of all nations

Matthew 28:19b

Paul Borthwick \\ Lexington, MA

Introduction: What is the Great Commission?

A pastor led the adult Sunday school on Missions Sunday. Throughout the class, he mentioned "the Great Commission," repeatedly. He described our church's role in the Great Commission. He explained how we're invested in the Great Commission. He encouraged his listeners to pray for our partners in the Great Commission. But he never explained what the Great Commission meant.

A young man, a newly committed follower of Jesus who had come to faith out of a totally unchurched background, sat through the class and took many notes. The pastor knew that this young fellow was new to faith, and in an effort to help the young man, the pastor asked, "So what do you think is the Great Commission?"

The new believer looked unsure, but he guessed. "I'm not sure, but given my experience in sales, I'd guess the Great Commission would be 30%. Ten percent would be good, 20% would be better, but 30% would be great!"

The pastor realized that Christian vocabulary does not translate to the unchurched person, so he took the man to the passage in our series — Matthew 28:16-20 — to explain Jesus' mandate to His followers.

Great Commission — or Great Commissions?

Matthew 28:16–20 is the passage that often includes the phrase "Great Commission" above it in our Bibles, but we need to remember that Jesus used similar words throughout the 40 days he walked the earth after His Resurrection. A look at all of the passages helps us to understand the bigger picture. Similar exhortations from Jesus can help us unpack the meaning of our focus today, "make disciples of all nations" (Matthew 28:19b).

We know that in the time between His Resurrection and His ascension into heaven, Jesus traveled and spoke to a variety of His followers in different contexts. The Gospel writers record these words in what we know as the Great Commission statements. In these words Jesus is making His last "before I go" wishes clear. In them, He is saying to all of His followers – including us – "remember this" or "if you don't remember anything else, remember this."

Our focus is on the most detailed of these commissions — Matthew 28:16-20 — but to set the bigger picture, we should see all of the commissions together. They appear at the end of each of the four Gospels (Matthew, Mark, Luke, and John), as well as just before Jesus' ascension recorded in Acts 1. Listen to the passages, and then we'll return to Matthew's record, and specifically Matthew 28:19b, in greater detail. Note in each reading the portions that specifically echo the "make disciples of all nations" theme.

We start in Matthew 28:18–20: "Jesus came to them and said, 'All authority in heaven and on earth has been given to me. Therefore go and *make disciples of all nations*, baptizing them in the name of the Father and of the Son and of the Holy Spirit, and teaching them to obey everything I have commanded you. And surely I am with you always, to the very end of the age' " (emphasis added).

Mark records it this way in Mark 16:15: He said to them, "*Go into all the world* and preach the good news to all creation" (emphasis added).

In the Gospel of Luke (Luke's first volume), he records it like this: "Then He opened their minds so they could understand the Scriptures. He told them, 'This is what is written: The Messiah will suffer and rise from the dead on the third day, and repentance and forgiveness of sins will be *preached in his name to all nations, beginning at Jerusalem.* You are witnesses of these things. I am going to send you what my Father has promised; but stay in the city until you have been clothed with power from on high' " (Luke 24:46–49, emphasis added).

Luke continues and geographically expands the "all nations" in Acts 1:8: "But you will receive power when the Holy Spirit comes on you; and *you will be my witnesses in Jerusalem, and in all Judea and Samaria, and to the ends of the earth"* (emphasis added).

In John, the Apostle records Jesus' words: "Again Jesus said, 'Peace be with you! *As the Father has sent me, I am sending you.'* And with that he breathed on them and said, 'Receive the Holy Spirit' " (John 20:21–22, emphasis added).

Combine these statements and the conclusion is unavoidable. Jesus wants His followers to go (John 20:21).

- To all nations (Matthew and Luke)
- To the entire creation (Mark)
- And to our homelands (Jerusalem), our regions (Judea), across cultures locally (Samaria), and cross-culturally globally (ends of the earth) (Acts).

Put another way, we who follow Jesus are called by Jesus to be *on mission.* Our mission is to share the Good News as witnesses, grow as disciples, live with Holy Spirit power, and invite every person into a relationship with Jesus. And who is Jesus' target audience? The whole world — every nation and ethnic group. But we are not alone. He promised that the Holy Spirit will be the source of our power; He assured us of His presence.

As we look at these words, keep Jesus' listeners in mind. Jesus gives all of these statements to people whose failure and denial of Christ is fresh in their minds. They had denied or abandoned Jesus hours or days before. They were not standing in front of Jesus hoping for a new challenge. They were bruised and ashamed of their cowardice. When He commands them to "make disciples of all nations," or "be my witnesses," or "preach the Gospel to everyone everywhere," I can imagine them thinking to themselves, "You have got to be kidding, Jesus. We couldn't even stand up for you right here in Jerusalem, and you're talking about the 'ends of the earth'?"

And don't forget, Jesus' audience was almost entirely Jewish. When Jesus said "all nations" He uses a Greek word that literally means "all ethnic groups." Jesus wasn't referring to some geo-political nation, He was referring to all the ethnic groups of the world. The disciples, in contrast to Jesus' global vision, gave evidence through their years with Jesus that they despised Samaritans and avoided the unclean Gentiles — both of whom represented the "all nations" or "to the ends of the earth" to which Jesus referred.

It's safe to say that all of Jesus' disciples were highly ethno-centric and resistant to the people to whom Jesus wanted to send them. They likely would have first understood phrases like "all nations" (Matthew and Luke), "all creation" (Mark), or "to the ends of the earth" (Acts) as referring to dispersed Jews all over the world. But when Jesus gets specific and mentions both Judea and *Samaria* (Acts), they would have known that Jesus was taking them outside their comfort zone. Samaritans were despised half-breeds that their parents had taught them to avoid.

Matthew 28:16–20 — Sent Out with Superlatives

Matthew 28:19b gives us a sense of not only the global nature of our mission as followers of Christ, but also the end result Jesus had in mind —— to make disciples. To enlarge our understanding of the mandate to "make disciples of all nations," it helps to realize that Matthew's Great Commission record builds on four superlatives.

The resurrected Jesus begins by establishing our *platform for outreach: His supreme authority*. "*All* authority" is His. Our commission into the world is not denominational or local church–based. It is not primarily motivated by human need nor by strategic opportunity. We're sent out by the authority of Jesus — and it's no small authority, it's ALL authority — in heaven and on earth. When Jesus says "authority," I imagine the disciples, who had seen His miracle-working powers already, immediately flashing to the realization that Jesus had just demonstrated God's authoritative power over death, and indeed the Roman government. *The grave could not hold Him.*

I imagine the picture Matthew describes with Jesus talking to His disciples. As He begins what we have recorded as Matthew 28:16–20, He stretches out His arms and says, "All authority in heaven and on earth has been given to me." I envision the disciples in awe as the daylight behind Jesus shone through the nail-pierced holes in His hands. All authority, indeed! Knowing that we stand on His authority gives us boldness to speak. It gives us courage because we realize the authority behind us is the power that raised Jesus from the dead. When we go in outreach and proclamation to others, we stand on the superlative authority of Jesus.

Jesus goes on to give the *content of our proclamation: teaching others to obey ALL that He taught.* As we are going into the world, we are supposed to teach people to obey ALL things that Jesus commanded. We cannot pick our favorite texts at the expense of the tough ones. Nor can we serve people just the sweet parts of biblical faith, a sort of "Christianity light." Our commission is to teach obedience to everything that Jesus taught and exemplified, starting with our own lives as disciples. We cannot avoid the teaching about standing strong in the face of hardship, the challenge to take up our cross daily, and the exhortation to forgive the people who have hurt us. We need Jesus' superlative authority to enable us to teach His superlative truth.

Then Jesus articulates the *destination of our outreach — ALL nations* (or all ethnic groups). We cannot focus just on the people who look like us or fit into our culturally specific enclave. Jesus wants no one to be left out. His superlative vision is for all the peoples on earth. With all the diverse ethnicities of the world in mind, our outreach takes us to our neighbors, but Jesus likewise opens our eyes to the Cambodian Buddhist woman at the supermarket, the international student from China whom we see on campus, the Muslim who owns the variety store, and the physically handicapped person that we might find easy to overlook. Jesus says, "God so loved *the world*, and I want you to love the world too."

The platform of Jesus' authority stands strong, but teaching "all things" and going to "all nations" seems overwhelming. To keep us from being intimidated by the challenge, Jesus closes with a *superlative promise* — *"I am with you ALWAYS."* In other words, Jesus is telling us that there's no place we can go that He won't go with us. He will give us the words to speak and the love we need to share. He'll be the One empowering our words, and He's the One who can break through to enlighten people's hearts.

We're sent out on a superlative mission by a supreme Lord. All His truth must be proclaimed. All people must have a chance to respond to His love. But don't worry: He's not just the supreme commander, He's also the supreme companion.

Matthew 28:19b — Make Disciples of All Nations

The superlatives in Matthew stand out. He bookends our tasks — making disciples of all nations and teaching disciples to obey all things — with the foundation of our mandate (all authority) and the assurance of His companionship along the way (I am with you always).

In Matthew's Gospel, Greek experts point out that the imperative is "make disciples" surrounded by three participles — as you are going, as you are teaching, as you are baptizing. In other words, Jesus assumes that we will be on the go — not just on some sort of official mission trip, but on our way to work, to the marketplace, to the neighborhood, to the school.

The imperative, "make disciples," presents us with the challenge. Our goal is not simply to make converts or to solicit evangelistic decisions. Our goal is to work with people to produce whole-hearted, integrated, obeying-all-things disciples of Jesus. The call to discipleship means a lifetime decision, and not just a calling to receive forgiveness and gain heavenly assurance.

The phrase *panta ta ethne* — all ethnicities — expands our mission beyond simply nations (i.e., geo-political entities that we see on our maps). The call identifies the discipling of all of the world's ethnic groups. So rather than thinking of India, for example, as one nation, Jesus calls us to disciple people from every one of India's more than 1,500 ethnic groups.

Jesus' words in Matthew identify His desire for the ethnic expansion of the Kingdom, which comes as a distinct challenge to the ethnocentric to whom Matthew was written. Like all of us, we can assume that they were okay with the idea of Jesus as Savior for *my* people, but what about those outside my socio-ethnic sphere?

Make Disciples of All Nations: Three Life Lessons

Taking our specific passage into account and enlarging our understanding by looking at parallel texts in the other Gospels and the Book of Acts, what's the application? In other words, what are we supposed to do with these words in terms of understanding how we should live? Consider three major themes related to Matthew 28:19b.

Lesson 1: A Mindset — Living as a sent person

The fact that the words "make disciples" is the primary imperative in the text reminds us that Jesus assumes that the life of discipleship has an active component: "as you are going, as you are baptizing, as you are teaching," to make disciples. Many refer to this as living a life of 24/7 availability to God.

As we are going into our communities, look for ways to invite others into a life of following Jesus. As we do our daily work, look for ways to glorify God and show the gospel through our lives. Be aware that "making disciples" is not primarily about bringing people to church; instead it is us going to them.

A woman enters her microbiology lab early on a Monday morning so that she can remember her Matthew 28 mandate. She walks slowly through the lab and prays over the work stations. Like Isaiah, she prays, "Here I am, Lord, send me" — to the Gujarati Hindu fellow; to the orthodox Christian lady who long ago became disillusioned with faith; to the co-workers from East Asia who have no apparent faith. She is there to do her work with excellence, but she is looking for opportunities to invite people to a life of following Jesus as disciples.

A student enters his high school and prays over the lockers of his classmates. He knows that this is where he is sent. He might end up later in life in Kathmandu reaching out to Tibetan or Bhutanese refugees, but today he's sent to the high school. His daily mindset of being sent has led to many evangelistic conversations, and he has encouraged other Christians to be bolder in their faith expression.

A retired couple walks around their 55+ community and prays quietly household by household. They have served in the past in Papua, New Guinea, and in Moldova, but now they know that this community is where they are presently sent. The prayer walks have resulted in new relationships, a neighborhood Bible study, and three friends who now come to church in an effort to understand Christian faith and grow as disciples.

Peter hustles busily to fulfill orders at the McDonalds where he works. Seeing him at a McDonalds in Cambridge, Massachusetts, is surprising when you discover that he has just graduated Harvard University with a master's degree. Ask Peter why he is there and he'll explain: "Well, I graduated in May but I went four months without finding a job, so I said to myself, 'I need some income to pay bills.' So this is where I've ended up — at least for now." But he refuses any pity. "Don't be sorry. God has sent me here. This place is giving me awesome opportunities to share my faith. I'm on a shift that includes a Buddhist guy from Sri Lanka, a Muslim fellow from Lebanon, a Hindu lady from India, and a fellow Christian from El Salvador. It's awesome. I get to be a global missionary to my co-workers while asking, 'Would you like fries with that?' " Peter is going to work (the 3–11 shift) with his eyes open to being on mission. His mindset of living as a sent person shaped the way he looked at his circumstances and the people around him.

The world into which God has sent us includes our neighborhood, our workplace, our friends, and natural contacts — our fellow students and our family. The person seated next to us on the bus or airplane, the person waiting in the unemployment line with us, or the homeless guy we walk by every day on the way to the office are all people to whom God sends us. Living as a sent person is a mindset: we hear Jesus' voice daily saying, "As you are going, I'm with you. Look for opportunities to invite others to a life of following Me."

Lesson 2: A Worldview — Don't leave anyone out!

In the phrase "all nations," we hear the heart of God for people outside of the community of faith. As the Bible affirms, God "wants all people to be saved and come to a knowledge of the truth" (1 Timothy 2:4).

In other words, our going or living as "sent" people is not limited to people just like us. Jesus sends us out cross-culturally and internationally. Remember the commissions? As we are going . . . the goal is all nations (*panta ta ethne*) or "all ethnicities" (Matthew 28:19; Luke 24:47). We start at home (our Jerusalem), but we don't stay there. Acts 1:8 helps us gain a fuller understanding of Jesus' statement about "all nations" in Matthew 28:

- To Jerusalem — our immediate surroundings, workplace, neighborhood, extended family, social contacts
- To Judea — our wider region, but basically similarly cultural and linguistic
- To Samaria — those who are geographically near but culturally distant, including those we have been taught to fear or even hate. Our Samaritans might be undocumented immigrants. Or perhaps they are prisoners or former prisoners. Some fear or hate people from other religions,

especially those whom we might assume are radical or extremists. And for many, the Samaritans are the LGBT community.

- To the ends of the earth. The Bible affirms that God blesses His people so that we in turn will bless the nations. The call to Abram affirms it in Genesis 12:1–3. The Psalmist reiterates it in Psalm 67. We followers of Jesus are called to be a light to the nations. Caring only about ourselves is "too small" for the purposes of God (see Isaiah 49:6). "Make disciples of all nations" calls us to grow in our willingness to cross cultures. God may call us to some of the more than 2 billion people on planet earth who have never been invited to believe in and respond to Jesus Christ as Savior unless someone crosses a culture to tell them.

But for all of us, the migration of people serves as God's wake-up call to start thinking cross-culturally now! A walk through almost any urban downtown will reveal the nations right there in front of us. Ask politely, "What language are you speaking?" and the response could come back: Dari (Afghanistan), Punjabi (India), Creole (Haiti), Urdu (Pakistan), Arabic, Spanish, Chinese, Mongolian, Armenian. You will lose count of the number of languages heard. And these people are not thousands of miles away. They are here! The God who "so loved the world" (John 3:16) has brought them here to hear the invitation to follow Jesus.

The worldview that understands that no one should be left out invites us to start learning about our neighbors, becoming friends, sharing meals. Building relationships with people from other countries starts with genuine interest, humble curiosity, and respectful initiative. And from these relationships, the steps toward following Jesus might begin. *Open your eyes to the world in our midst.* Start the conversation. Ask a question. Don't be afraid. Look for the opportunities. When we see someone who doesn't fit into our culture or social group, don't run away. Reach out! God brought them here for us to love, serve, and invite to Jesus. We're on the go to do our part to expand the Kingdom of Christ to every *ethne*, every people group. Jesus sends us out — even across cultures — to give everyone an invitation, not just to make some sort of momentary decision, but rather:

- To become disciples with a living, vital relationship with God
- To become identified with Christ and the Christian community
- To join the Christian community in living as people sent into the world empowered by the Holy Spirit and assured of Jesus' presence

Lesson 3: An Assurance — Jesus is always with us

Even though our focus is on the phrase "make disciples of all nations," we need to remember the fuller context of this commission so that we can go into the world and reach out across cultures with courage. Matthew 28:19–20 calls us to a changed view of ourselves: we are sent into the world. The Great Commission sends us out so that every person understands Jesus' invitation to a relationship with Him. But we don't go alone. Jesus repeatedly reminds us:

- I am with you always to the end of time (Matthew 28:20).
- I'll send you the Holy Spirit (Luke 24:49).
- And My Spirit will be your source of power to be My witnesses (Acts 1:8).

It's too tempting to look at the world in fear. Jesus speaks and says, "Don't be afraid. I am with you ALWAYS." The dynamite power of the Holy Spirit that raised Jesus from the dead is ours! We need it because living to make disciples can be overwhelming. The needs and hurts of people can push us to tears. We need it because going to the ends of the earth, or to the family down the street, or to the guy in the apartment down the hall, can be scary. In the face of all of life's unknowns, Jesus says, "I am with you." In the face of fearful, out-of-control situations, Jesus says, "be strong and courageous." When we call, He is there.

Dr. Peter Kuzmic serves as professor at Gordon-Conwell Theological Seminary and President of the Evangelical Theological Seminary in Osijek, Croatia. He grew up under the pressures of Yugoslavian Socialism and Soviet Communism. He stayed with his family in the former Yugoslavia during the Serbian-Bosnian war of 1994. He knows police interrogations and huddling in the stairway, covering his children while bombs fell nearby. Yet he also knows that Jesus' promise to be with us always is real. He knows that *all authority* ultimately resides in the risen Savior. In his words, "We don't need to live in fear. The final word of history will not come from Washington or Moscow or Beijing; it will come from the Lord of history and the Lord of heaven."[1]

Conclusion

As you are going, make disciples. And don't limit yourself to your own people, your own culture, or your own nation. Go with the accompanying power of God and assured presence of Jesus. The resurrected Lord of heaven is always with us. The One who says "Go into all the world and preach the gospel to all creation" (Mark 16:15) promises to be with us always.

Addendum

I first met Ben when he was a junior in high school. He came from a Christian family, but he was looking for a mentor to help him apply his faith to his real, day-to-day teenage life. He served one summer as my intern while I led the Missions program at our church.

The greatest discipling influence I had on his life was involving him cross-culturally in outreach. He went out each summer in service with student ministry in Uganda. This cross-cultural service so stirred his faith that it expanded his witness throughout the school year in his own country.

After graduation, Ben decided to go to Uganda to serve for five years with the Ugandan equivalent of InterVarsity Christian

---

1. Dr. Peter Kuzmic, Lecture in Cross-Cultural Studies, Gordon-Conwell Theological Seminary, South Hamilton, MA, June, 2002.

Fellowship. We walked with him through cross-cultural commu-nication issues, through the crisis of a friend with HIV, and later through a cross-cultural marriage.

Now, 20 years married, Ben and his wife divide their impact between student ministry in Boston and service in Uganda. The role that my wife and I have played has been primarily as encour-agers. Ben would say the greatest discipling effect of their lives has been our own example — serving, ministering, and disci-pling across cultures.

8

Baptizing them in the name of the Father and of the Son and of the Holy Spirit

Matthew 28:19c

Scott Taube \\ Portland, ME

This past summer has been the greatest summer in the history of Eastpoint Christian Church (EP). We have seen over 2,000 people attend each week in MAINE! We get pumped about that because it's an indication of the hunger for the gospel of Jesus in a predominantly unreached state. It's evidence of the desire to KNOW Jesus and crave the community of Jesus. I just want to celebrate that with you. We're taking a few weeks to talk about what we do every Sunday. Perhaps those looking from the outside in would naturally wonder or ask, "Why do you do that every Sunday? Why do you meet? Why do you take communion? Why do you sing songs as a group? Why do people give money every week? Why do you pray for one, and in preparation for next week's 'baptism Sunday,' why do you baptize people?" We baptize people every Sunday and throughout the week — whenever someone is ready to respond as part of their decision to follow Jesus.

Over the past couple of years in the month of September, we have also chosen a Sunday for those who have been thinking about baptism, or who have gone through a summer Starting Point group, and are ready. Jesus said, "Go and make disciples of all nations, baptizing them . . . and teaching them to obey everything I have commanded you" (Matt. 28:19–20). We never stop encouraging people to identify with Jesus in baptism. We've witnessed as many as 77 people on a single Sunday, and not long ago, 84 people over a couple of Sundays. So we want you to be faithful to Jesus in baptism because He invites us to identify with Him there. It's an amazing connection with Jesus!

Why do we baptize people at Eastpoint?

So why do we do it? Where does it come from? What's the significance? I hope to answer as much of that as possible. A lot of people most likely have some kind of opinion on baptism. What we learn from history and what the Bible teaches will hopefully clear up any confusion on the subject and help you understand why Jesus wants you to be baptized. It's all His idea, and to be clear, we want you to be baptized, too. But you need to know why. If you already have been, perhaps this chapter will help you in explaining it to others.

You'll notice in the New Testament stories of those who became followers of Jesus, except for a couple of supernatural occasions, being baptized was something they did almost immediately as part of their response to accepting His message. If you find it strange that we participate in this practice because it seems like a strange ritual to jump into a pool of water and have someone lay you back like you're being buried in the water, then lift you up like you're coming back to life (and you sort of are), consider other strange practices that we don't call strange. For instance, once a year we invite friends and neighbors to gather and we don little hats that point straight to the sky with elastic bands that run under our chins. Then, we place a number of fire sticks on a sponge-like platform and dance around singing to someone who has just become another year older. Happy Birthday! It sounds absolutely normal to all of us. And baptism was a very normal response for those in the first century who heard the gospel of Jesus. Baptism has been practiced ever since, even though some have changed the mode, the method, and some have distorted Jesus' plan altogether. People are being baptized all over the world. Every day of the year there is most likely someone being baptized, and on specific days, hundreds and even thousands are being baptized as a part of their decision to follow Jesus. Baptism, the picture, the image, the act is indeed a death, a burial, and a resurrection to new life.

I have to say, it can bring up some emotion, even controversy, for a number of people. Sometimes, Christians from various backgrounds want to argue about mode or method. They wonder, Is it important? Is it necessary? Is it essential? Does baptism save you? I've never heard it to be a struggle for those who are being drawn to Jesus as they listen to His message, or read His or Paul's instruction, or observe baptism practiced. They often draw the conclusion on their own that it is something Jesus asks of them, something that connects them to Him, and they're willing to do it. Pretty simple overall, and that's how we see it too. Just listen to Jesus. He said it was important. We'll share when Jesus Himself was baptized. We'll witness it throughout the early church. Then you can draw your own conclusions and make your own decision. Jesus included baptizing people as part of the commission given to the disciples before leaving the earth to be with His Father. It's not confusing or unclear.

Matthew 28:16–20

> Then the eleven disciples went to Galilee, to the mountain where Jesus had told them to go. When they saw him, they worshiped him; but some doubted. Then Jesus came to them and said, "All authority in heaven and on earth has been given to me. Therefore go and make disciples of all nations, baptizing them in the name of the Father and of the Son and of the Holy Spirit, and teaching them to obey everything I have commanded you. And surely I am with you always, to the very end of the age."

One of the reasons we baptize people at EP is because Jesus told us to. He thought it was important enough to include it in the final instructions given to His disciples before they headed out into the world to share Him with others. In fact, Jesus thought it was so important, that He was baptized Himself. We're leading up to that. First let me just tell you where the idea came from and what it literally means.

Our word baptize came from the Greek word *baptize* — *meaning wash, soak, plunge, immerse or dip.* It was used in such common practices as washing dishes or dipping soup. So how did this common word of the day, *baptizo*, take on theological meaning? Here's a little more history for us. Between the Old Testament and the time Jesus came to usher the gospel into the world (the bringing of a New Covenant where people would no longer be under the laws of Moses), Jesus would fulfill the law in Himself by making us righteous through Him. This was not by our own merit or performance. This was a period of about 400 years when God was silent. During that time, Gentiles (non-Jewish people like most of us), would visit Palestine, Jerusalem, and Judea, where the Jewish people lived. The Gentiles thought the Jewish people were great because they only had one God, which was not as confusing as having many gods like so many of them had. Many wanted to become Jewish. Long story short, some of the Jewish leaders came up with a system by which the Gentiles could do that. The process included men needing to have a little surgery — circumcision. Don't ask me why that little ceremony was something God included, but one thing we know is that if it's done on the eighth day of a child's life, it's not quite as memorable as . . . well, it's slightly uncomfortable to talk about now. But that too could be a rather strange practice, eh? In addition to circumcision, the Gentiles would have to share in following other things if they were to become Jews.

- A covenant meal that reflects the Passover
- Acknowledge and surrender to the old covenant law of Moses
- Memorize parts of the law
- Make a sacrifice

- Take part in a ceremonial washing. This was something you did alone. It represented a cleansing of gentile-ness, a cleansing of sin, and a complete surrender to God, our God, the one true God.

When the ceremonial washing took place, they used the natural word *baptizo*, or a Hebrew equivalent, of course. The Hebrew word was *mikveh*, meaning to immerse in water. Water is actually an important theme in Scripture. Phrases referring to water are common, such as "a river that flows from the throne of God" or Jesus speaking about "living water." The Hebrew word *mikveh* has the same interpretation as *baptizo*. In addition, let me share something I love to share at this point, something I've shared in the past.

Jesus is not introducing something new here. He's taking something OLD and giving it NEW meaning. *Mikveh*, or *baptizo*, was very familiar to the Jewish people. It happened before people would enter the temple as a ritual cleansing, part of a ceremonial washing. When I was in Jerusalem, we saw the remnants. Some of the baptistries or mikvehs still hold water around or outside the temple. Many of them have two sets of stairs. You enter into the water through one set, and when you are cleansed, you come up out of the water through a different set of stairs. Jesus takes this old ceremony of spiritual cleansing and brings new meaning to baptism. It still means to dip, plunge, or immerse, but it takes on an even greater meaning: to be baptized with Jesus, to be immersed into Him, or in His name, which moves us beyond physical water — way beyond what water could ever do. It's more an image of plunging our whole life, our whole self into Jesus, being covered, immersed in, washed by Jesus. He becomes our righteousness, our hope, our salvation, literally "our everything," when you make Him your Lord. Listen to what Paul writes:

> Don't you know that all of us who were baptized into Christ Jesus were baptized into his death? We were therefore buried with him through baptism into death in order that, just as Christ was raised from the

dead through the glory of the Father, we too may live a new life (Romans 6:3–4).

A real participation with Jesus

Jesus uses the physical participation of baptism to both symbolize and allow us to participate in His death, burial, and Resurrection, all of which He did for us in order to save us. In baptism you participate in all of it. It's not merely a ritual, but a place of identifying with Jesus. If you've been baptized, you may not have understood then as much as you might today, but today can make you appreciate your baptism that much more — that it wasn't just a ritual or ceremony, but a real participation with Jesus, in death, putting our old self to death, burying our old self, past sin being raised clean, yet fully dependent upon Jesus to be our righteousness, simply because we cannot be righteous without Him. Since drawing near to Jesus, seeking to imitate Jesus and be like Him, and growing in recognition that life in Jesus is always better, then following Him even in baptism allows us to experience Him more, draw near in yet another way. I believe He honors that. He blesses that.

Jesus was baptized

Another reason we baptize people at EP is the example of Jesus Himself. About A.D. 30, a prophet named John came out of the wilderness preaching to the Jewish people, "Repent, repent!" He was calling for an acknowledgment of personal sinfulness, and a need to be cleansed of it. Repentance is a good thing! He came announcing that God was going to be doing something new, and that "something" would be coming through Jesus. He was preparing for the coming of the Savior of the world, the promised Messiah, Jesus the Christ. He told the people they needed to repent and be baptized. Someone greater than he was coming. Someone whose sandals he wasn't worthy to untie. People from all over came, listened, were moved by the message about their personal sin, convicted as we should be because we all have it, and they were baptized for the forgiveness of sin. It was a cleansing that accompanied repentance that God would honor in any who were obedient.

John baptized so many people that he received the nickname "John the Baptist," or "John the Baptizer." It was something that had never been done before; it was new. The rest of the story is that one day as John was baptizing he looked up, saw Jesus and said, "Behold the lamb of God who takes away the sins of the world." Then Jesus walked right up to John and said, "I need to be baptized by you." John of course deferred and said something like, NO way! If anything at all, I need to be baptized by you, Jesus. But Jesus insisted it was necessary for John to baptize Him because He knew it would fulfill all righteousness, and that if people watched, if it was told, it would confirm the message of John the Baptizer, a baptism of repentance, and open the door for a baptism that Jesus would bring — a baptism that would include the Holy Spirit of God, the presence of God, and a grace that only Jesus can give. (Paraphrased from Matthew 3:1–2)

Listen to how John the Baptizer describes it in Matthew 3:11.

> I baptize you with water for repentance. But after me comes one who is more powerful than I, whose sandals I am not worthy to carry. He will baptize you with the Holy Spirit and fire.

In spite of John's sense of unworthiness to baptize Jesus, He did as Jesus asked. Take a look at what happens in Matthew 3:16:

> As soon as Jesus was baptized, he went up out of the water. At that moment heaven was opened, and he saw the Spirit of God descending like a dove and alighting on him.

So with the coming of Jesus and the baptism, through our surrender, repentance of sin, our confession of Jesus as Lord, our baptism, our immersion not just in water, but into Jesus, allowing Him to pour over and into our very lives, we receive the gift of God's Spirit. It's the same Spirit of God that came and rested on Jesus at His baptism. It's the same Spirit we receive when we humble ourselves, accepting that we can't save ourselves, that we need Jesus to wash away our sin. It's the same response of the Jewish people who heard Peter preach, the people who put Jesus on the Cross, when they discovered what they had truly done. In addition, Acts 2:37–38 says:

> When the people heard this, they were cut to the heart and said to Peter and the other apostles, "Brothers, what shall we do?"
>
> Peter replied, "Repent and be baptized, every one of you, in the name of Jesus Christ for the forgiveness of your sins. And you will receive the gift of the Holy Spirit."

So just to review:

1. Jesus submits to His Father's authority and is baptized by John, at which time God's Spirit comes down upon Jesus and He is divinely revealed as the Son of God.

2. Jesus fulfills the law. It is now through life lived in Jesus that the Jews and all people of the world will come to know the Father.

3. Jesus gives and sets the example of baptism for us to follow.

It's an example that has been followed for 2,000 years. There's no question that anyone can follow that example. Anyone can acknowledge sin, repent, confess faith in Jesus, and be baptized — even the most distant, or those with the hardest of hearts. Look at the Apostle Paul when he met Jesus on the road to Damascus. Paul was traveling on his way to persecute and kill Christians, then Jesus appeared to Paul in a blinding light, literally. It blinded Paul. Jesus convinced Paul of who He is, Paul placed his own faith in Jesus, and look at the rest of his response. God called a messenger, Ananias, to go and pray for Paul who was still blind. Ananias placed his hands on Paul and here's what happened after he prayed.

> Immediately, something like scales fell from Saul's eyes, and he could see again. He got up and was baptized, and after taking some food, he regained his strength (Acts 9:18–19).

The truth is, we don't want to be extremists who make baptism something it isn't, and we don't want to be minimalists teaching that it has little value or is optional. Jesus placed high value on it by doing it Himself and commanding His disciples to baptize as they go into the world and make more disciples. It's part of our response to accepting Jesus and we don't want you to miss it. It's an honor to Jesus and He honors you and me for being faithful. He always blesses faithfulness.

Later in Acts 22 Paul was arrested. While being taken into custody, he was given permission to speak to the Jewish people who rioted against him, so he told his whole story of conversion which included meeting Jesus and how Ananias came to pray over him, and he filled in a few details we didn't get earlier:

> Then he said: "The God of our ancestors has chosen you to know his will and to see the Righteous One and to hear words from his mouth. You will be his witness to all people of what you have seen and heard. And now what are you waiting for? Get up, be baptized and wash your sins away, calling on his name" (Acts 22:14–16).

I don't know what you think after reading all of this, seeing it for yourself in the life and ministry of Jesus, and in the life and ministry of His Apostles in the early church. It was the response of many people to the offer of salvation in the churches Paul planted. If after all of that, you say, "I can see that Jesus wants me to be baptized, to participate in that very personal sacrifice of His death, burial, and Resurrection for me, I want to honor Him,

I want to be faithful to the request He asks of me." The church can joyfully offer that to you. We can do it at any time. But don't wait! This is important if you know the Holy Spirit is speaking to you, or your heart is moved by the truth of Jesus.

Addendum

I met Tim on a Sunday when he came in with his girlfriend. He looked as cynical as anyone I had ever seen coming through our doors. Slouching in his seat, his hat was pulled down over his forehead, leaving his squinty eyes that matched the scowl on the rest of his face revealed. That was every Sunday for months. One day I got a call that Tim was on a three-day binge in a local motel. He was a long-time alcoholic. I took two others with me and went to the motel. There was an empty half-gallon jug of bourbon on one side of the bed, an almost empty one on the other. We got him ready and headed to Wendy's. It would be days of getting him sober. During the visitations while Tim was in rehab, we shared that Jesus loves him and wants to save him. He found it hard to believe but was definitely listening. It wasn't a conversion story that was always up and to the right. He failed many times. We never gave up on him. Eventually, he gave his life to Jesus. He said there were four of us who came to the hotel room that day. There were only three. We know who the fourth one was. His baptism was truly a "new birth." Two weeks ago, I attended his 12-year sobriety celebration. He's been leading, discipling, and baptizing other addicts for the past 12 years as part of his own recovery. God is GREAT!

9

Teaching them to obey everything I have commanded you

Matthew 28:20a

Larry Strondak \\ Westbrook, ME

Then the eleven disciples went to Galilee, to the mountain where Jesus had told them to go. When they saw him they worshiped him; but some doubted. Then Jesus came to them and said, "All authority in heaven and on earth has been given to me. Therefore go and make disciples of all nations, baptizing them in the name of the Father and of the Son and of the Holy Spirit, and teaching them to obey everything I have commanded you. And surely I am with you always, to the very end of the age" (Matthew 28:16–20).

The latest Robin Hood movie had just opened in theaters and I was inspired to purchase a recurved bow and begin archery lessons. Convinced that I could shoot with ease and accuracy, just like Robin of Locksley, I enthusiastically paced out 50 yards and let my first arrow fly. . . . To my disappointment, the arrow missed by a long shot. My instructor laughed and jibed, "We're not going to find that one." We moved only 10 yards from the target, and I was instructed in proper technique. The teacher advised me to take three steps back once I was able to get three arrows in the bullseye. Thank God for my instructor. Left on my own, my excitement and investment in archery would have ended in disappointment and frustration. Instead, within a few short months, I was able to hit a moving target accurately at 25 yards. Eventually, I was helping my friends achieve the same results.

Any worthwhile endeavor requires inspiration, commitment, careful instruction, and practice. Lacking in one of these areas can cause a person to become completely disinterested, lose hope, and eventually give up. It's one thing when we are talking about archery, but it's entirely tragic when it comes to following Jesus and remaining faithful. Every great plan begins with inspiration, and inspiration is essential in pushing us forward as we advance. But excitement and enthusiasm should move toward healthy stages of development. Imagine if our teachers relied too much on inspiration. What if instead of teaching you the theory of multiplication and instructing you to study your tables, your math teacher pumped you up telling you they believed in your ability to do multiplication? "You've been created by God with a mind that is endowed with the power of mathematics! Multiplication is powerful! Useful! Life changing! Now go do multiplication!" You might leave completely motivated to change the world through multiplication, but without knowledge and practice, you'll just bumble around in trial and error.

We understand that we need to learn, practice, and grow in things such as school and sports. In the same way, the Scriptures teach us that God has given us leaders to equip "his people for works of service, so that the body of Christ may be built up until we all reach unity in the faith and in the knowledge of the Son of God and become mature, attaining to the whole measure of the fullness of Christ" (Ephesians 4:12–13). Jesus wants us to grow in maturity to our full potential as disciples.

But maturity doesn't happen overnight. It would be scary if it did. Imagine putting a baby to sleep and waking to find a teenager. Yikes! It would actually be dangerous. Likewise, maturity comes with time, experience, practice, and patience. Yes, there are miraculous jumps along the way where the Holy Spirit intercedes in supernatural ways, and He gives us wisdom and insight. But this doesn't necessarily bring maturity. Even the most brilliant and gifted children aren't necessarily mature.

As we dig deeper into the gospel of Jesus Christ, we see that God has a plan for our spiritual formation that is . . .

- Energized by supernatural power
- Rooted in Scripture (that's where we find the teachings of Jesus)
- Grounded in healthy practices
- Empowered through community

Energized by Supernatural Power

Whenever we start talking about supernatural power, our ears perk up. When we hear about amazing things, we are often curious and a bit skeptical, yet many of us have experiences that we cannot explain because they are beyond human comprehension. First and foremost, the source of positive supernatural power is the working of God through His Son Jesus Christ in conjunction with the Holy Spirit. We have access to this power through the grace of God as we place our faith in Jesus. Faith isn't merely intellectual, it's relational and it's based on trust. I recently purchased an automobile and I gave the dealer $10,000 cash because I had faith that he would turn over the car and title to me. I'm not going to give $10,000 to just any schmo who comes to my door with a promise. My auto dealer has a reputation for reliability, and I've built a relationship with him. Likewise, faith has to do with trust and is at the heart of godly obedience.

As we come to know Christ Jesus, we begin to trust Him and His teaching. Eventually we come to believe that He is the Messiah, the Son of the living God, and we are faced with an important faith decision. Will we act on this belief? Will we commit to proclaim Jesus as Lord and be baptized as a sign of that committed relationship? Just like a ring is a sign of a marriage commitment, so baptism is a sign of our commitment with Jesus. Additionally, we are promised a supernatural relational gift.

"Repent and be baptized, every one of you, in the name of Jesus Christ for the forgiveness of your sins. And you will receive the gift of the Holy Spirit" (Acts 2:38).

The Holy Spirit binds Himself to us and helps us to follow Jesus, to remember and obey His teachings, encourages us in times of trouble, comforts us in distress, gives us courage in the face of adversity, gifts us to do the work of God, intercedes for us before God, and transforms our very character to become more like Jesus. How can we live in Christ without the Holy Spirit? The Spirit is influencing us right at this moment to have faith and act in accordance with God's will. You probably feel His presence moving you to align with God in worship, prayer, and to walk in faithful obedience.

Rooted in Scripture

The Holy Spirit is always moving us toward alignment with Scripture. In fact, that's how we can discern the presence of the Spirit from other voices. The Holy Spirit will never lead you to disobey God or compromise convictions. Jesus cares deeply about the motivation of the heart that moves us toward obedience.

Obedience to Scripture is a vital aspect of discipleship, but it must always be superseded by a love for God and others (John 13:34–35; 1 Corinthians 13:1–4). Our growth as disciples of Jesus must be approached as a relational opportunity rather than a dogmatic enterprise. Consequently, a love for God and others must flow through every aspect of our spiritual teaching and practices.

Humans are hardwired by God to share what they love. As Jesus says, "Out of the overflow of the heart, the mouth speaks" (Luke 6:45; Berean). Additionally, passion and enthusiasm are infectious. Our primary reason for sharing the joy we feel in Jesus is that we can't help it; we just love Jesus so much! And this love is contagious.

When the resurrected Jesus spent time with disciples on the road to Emmaus they replied, "Were not our hearts burning within us while he talked with us on the road and opened the

Scriptures to us?" (Luke 24:32). They were so excited about their experience that they traveled through the night to share with others what had happened. This is a beautiful illustration of the type of motivation that is at the core of our spiritual development.

Furthermore, Jesus commissions us to make disciples; His followers model this for us, and then urge us to become diligent in continuing this process. The Gospel of Matthew closes with Jesus commissioning His Apostles stating:

> All authority in heaven and on earth has been given to me. Therefore go and make disciples of all nations, baptizing them in the name of the Father and of the Son and of the Holy Spirit, and teaching them to obey everything I have commanded you. And surely I am with you always, to the very end of the age" (Matt. 28:18–20).

Here, the disciples receive a basic template for spiritual development beginning with hearing the gospel, progressing to commitment and baptism, then continuing with instruction and obedience. It should be noted that people are discipled *to* conversion, not simply after conversion. This is well illustrated in Jesus' ministry (John 1–2; Luke 5:1–11). We see through the gospels that the disciples were following Jesus and listening to Him some time before they placed their faith in Him. Consequently, spiritual formation begins before conversion and continues afterward.

In the first chapters of the Book of Acts we see this process modeled by the Apostles and early disciples as they devoted themselves to the core practices of teaching, community, prayer, generosity, hospitality, and evangelism (Acts 2:42–47). Luke repeatedly emphasized these elements and revealed a fruitful progression of healthy spiritual formation in both the church at large and in the lives of individuals. The church grew in numbers and in leadership. Men like Barnabas and Philip were the product of a discipleship process that they passed on as they were sent to plant new congregations.

Grounded in Healthy Practices

> In order to "learn God" and cultivate intimacy with God, human persons need guidance and a guide. The need for guidance is the reason Christian spiritual teachers have, for centuries, nurtured and cultivated practices of spiritual direction and formation. — Kay Northcutt[1]

God has always used people to deliver His redemptive message and train others in following His ways. As Parrett mentions in the above-quoted book, this is God's mission for parents (Deuteronomy 6:7) and also for spiritual directors (1 Peter 5:2). The principle of teaching, preaching, and imitation is demonstrated in both the Old and New Testaments. It would be great if the Holy Spirit miraculously downloaded knowledge and ability, but this rarely happens. Instead we listen, watch, practice, and learn from those who teach us. For this reason, we must carefully consider the people and sources that influence us.

It is right for us to look to the Scriptures first when searching for reliable principles in forming and developing healthy disciples of Jesus. Among faithful Christians, scriptural authority and direction should inform and influence above all other sources. God has also gifted us with a rich legacy of exemplary believers who have gone before us and fervently pursued a relationship with Christ. Additionally, there have been breakthroughs in education, science, and technology that help us to better understand the ways that people learn, grow, adapt, and change (see graph).

In a world of competing influences, it is important to prioritize sources of information because they do not speak to us with the same authority. The Wesleyan Quadrilateral is very helpful when weighing the influence of different sources in order to consider how we view issues and practice our faith as Christ followers. Before adopting influence and practices, it is wise to evaluate them, giving the most authority to Scripture, second to tradition,

1. Kay Northcutt, *Kindling Desire for God: Preaching as Spiritual Direction* (Minneapolis, MN: Fortress Press, 2009), Kindle 208.

Experience

Reason

Tradition

Scripture

third to reason, and last to experience.[2] Currently, our culture seems to be turning these influences upside down with experience taking the greatest weight in determining both conviction and practice. This has produced an environment that is conducive to moral decay and false teaching within the church. Incorporating and teaching a clear prioritization as we screen influences must become a foundational element of spiritual formation.

Although cultural clashes are inevitable, they provide an opportunity for the church to distinguish itself and glorify God by demonstrating that "the manifold wisdom of God should be made known to the rulers and authorities in the heavenly realms, according to his eternal purpose that he accomplished in Christ Jesus our Lord" (Ephesians 3:10–11). It is good to be relatable when we communicate the gospel, but Christians must beware not to conform to secular morays in an effort to appear relevant and engaging. The early church glorified God through its contrast rather than conformity.

People do not simply osmose the character of Christ, and without a clear plan, most people will be tossed around in a sea of influences like a ship without a rudder. Understanding true

2. D.G. Bloesch, *A Theology of Word and Spirit: Authority and Method in Theology* (Downers Grove, IL: IVP, 2005), p. 208–209.

discipleship requires us to recognize that there is a process to learning that involves teaching, watching, and practicing. In developing a Christ-like relationship with God and others we are striving to cultivate the profound disposition of the soul that is attentive to spiritual subtleties. This is a divinely empathic quality that is a combination of emotional and spiritual intelligence.

Most cultures have practices that align with the teachings of Jesus and some that don't. Americans align well in our value for compassion for the needy and our desire for justice, but we are lacking in our understanding of sexual purity and violence. We watch shows and movies that present relational practices that are completely antithetic to the teachings of Jesus. In our Core Values Class we talk about God's counterintuitive plan for sexuality and generosity. When it comes to sexuality, God has given us this gift to be exclusively enjoyed in a loving relationship between a man and woman in the context of a marriage relationship. When I share this, I receive some stunned looks, as if this is an impossible task. But we must realize that Christian chastity has been practiced by our brothers and sisters throughout history. Moreover, in many places in the world, the vast majority of men and woman abstain from sex before marriage because of social reasons that have nothing to do with faith. It can be done!

Those who choose to follow Jesus are a new creation, and it is amazing how young adults in our congregation come out of a worldly view of sexual relations and adopt the values of Jesus. These are producing amazing fruit in healthy friendships that develop into committed and faithful relationships. By demonstrating that we can be faithful to God in sexuality before marriage, we establish a firm foundation of fidelity within marriage. God has a purpose for purity that develops character in profound ways.

Recent scientific research in the fields of medicine, education, and sociology often attest to the importance of ancient practices of spiritual formation. For instance, recent studies demonstrate that brain structure in young adults is changed to become more conducive to learning when we are in healthy social environments.[3] As Christians, we are not called to resist technology but to use it righteously to enhance spiritual development. When we combine ancient wisdom and modern technology, they can enhance our understanding in ways we can only imagine.

Empowered through Community

Jesus taught His disciples in community because that is the way we are created to learn. Most of the gospel teachings are set in the context of Jesus interacting with individuals or groups of people while enjoying meals, traveling, and participating in community events. Even when Jesus addresses individuals, it is often in the company of others who are benefiting from what is said and taught. This pattern continues as we read about the early church in the Book of Acts and in the teachings of the Apostles.

> Day after day, in the temple courts and from house
> to house, they never stopped teaching and proclaiming
> the good news that Jesus is the Messiah (Acts 5:42).

The church is designed to function like a family where we learn foundational and essential skills and habits while we strive to love God and others. I can honestly say that this is how I learned 99% of Jesus' teachings. I learned to pray by listening to others pray and imitating them. I learned to read and understand the Scriptures by watching other Christians do this in a small group. I learned to be generous, compassionate, discerning, and caring while in the presence of devoted followers of Jesus. Although I sometimes gleaned information from books, articles, and videos, I learned to practice faith in Jesus by watching others.

I remember the first time I was asked to pray in a group. My immediate question was . . . "Out loud?" The answer was just as obvious and humorous . . . "Of course out loud, how else will we hear you and pray together?" I can still recall awkwardly

---

3. Luciane R Piccolo, Emily C Merz, and Kimberly G Noble, "School Climate Is Associated with Cortical Thickness and Executive Function in Children and Adolescents," *Developmental Science* 22.1 (2018), Wiley Online Library.

expressing my thoughts and heart to God and finishing with, "This is Larry signing off." The group's response was genuine encouragement with high-fives and a side note that we usually close by saying, "in Jesus name. Amen."

This is honestly how I learned to pray! I'm so glad I was part of a very accepting and encouraging group that allowed me to genuinely learn without the pressure to be perfect. Once, I was asked to lead a small group of about 30 people in a celebration of the Lord's Supper. I got so nervous during the event that I apologized in the middle of the service in prayer and ran outside of the building. Some friends caught up with me and encouraged me to come back in saying, "It really wasn't as bad as you thought. We all know that you wanted to honor God by doing a good job and simply got nervous. You should come in and finish. It will be good for you and everyone else." I ended up coming back into the room to applause and smiles. Strangely, upon returning I wasn't nervous at all. This became a teachable moment for everyone present.

We have great groups within the church. Some hang back from joining a group because of fear of awkwardness and embarrassment, but I want to urge you not to be afraid. We are all simply striving to follow Jesus and help each other along the way. Even as a more seasoned Christian, I learn lessons from new disciples, and I am reminded that sincere love of God and others is the goal of our faith. After following Jesus for over 30 years, it is still exciting to hear faith stories from young Christians who are filled with enthusiasm and the grace of God.

Invitation

It is important for us to understand that learning to follow the teachings of Jesus has an end goal. The goal of obedience is obtaining a maturity that involves the transformation of our character into the character of Christ. Building character takes time, perseverance, consistency in practice, and lots of prayer. Additionally, there is a lot of trial and error in this process because one

way that the Lord develops His character in us is through struggle and even suffering. Think about it — the only way we learn
patience is by wrestling with waiting. The way we learn honesty
is struggling with the cost of being truthful. The way we learn
meekness is by restraining our power, resisting the temptation to
manipulate and force our agenda. The way we learn to love is by
caring enough to sacrifice our time, resources, and energies for
the sake of others.

Character is very important to Jesus in establishing His Kingdom here and in the life to come. Obedience matters because
character matters. We are saved by grace through faith, and because of that we will enter God's eternal Kingdom. The Gospels
also lead us to believe that we will be commended, admonished,
and placed within eternity according to our faithful character.
That's a sobering thought.

The stakes are high. God is calling this generation to "live up
to what we have attained" (Philippians 3:16). We have been giv-
en an unparalleled set of resources with more access to information than any other time in history. Christ has passed the torch of
faith to us, and it is our responsibility, with the help of the Holy
Spirit, to enliven the souls of today.

I want to encourage you to step into a relational obedience
that builds character through grace — an obedience that is energized by supernatural power, rooted in the Scriptures, grounded
in healthy practices, and empowered through community.

Perhaps today is the day you commit to following Jesus and
step into obedience. I want to invite you to celebrate that through
baptism. Maybe you've slipped into some unhealthy practices.
Make a decision to repent, get back on track, and engage in a
group.

If you're a seasoned disciple, the Lord needs you to help teach
and train His people to obey. Jesus has poured the richness of His
grace into you. It's time to rise and become a servant-leader. You
don't need to know everything, just pass along what Jesus has
commanded you. And here's the promise — Jesus WILL be with
us until the very end!

Addendum

Example of Faithful Obedience

Scott had hit a middle-age slump and was looking for excitement. He had been married to his wife, Colleen, for over 25 years, had a wonderful son, Connor, and a successful business, but Scott felt bored and discontent. His wife had a flirtatious, attractive friend who always affirmed his ambitions and affections. She was a willing partner in a seduction and affair that was eventually discovered by Colleen. Scott was torn and wouldn't cut off the affair, so Colleen asked him to leave.

After a short time, the affair imploded, as they often do. Scott found himself depressed, lonely, and growing hard-hearted. He lost all joy in life and began to slip into cynicism and despair. Sometimes Christians would come into Scott's shop to purchase equipment, and they would talk about church, Jesus, and life. One day he overheard three separate conversations about our church. Curious, he went online and found the times and location of the services. The next Sunday was his first worship service since he was a child. The message was on the destruction of sin and the opportunity for repentance and grace through Jesus. As Scott listened, he felt hope flood back into his life. The hope presented was different from a pep talk or a self-help program. It was rooted in a relational commitment to follow Jesus. This was a supernatural hope that was coming from a source outside of himself.

After service he rushed to see his wife, Colleen, and begged her to come to church with him next week. Colleen reluctantly agreed, and they awkwardly worshiped together the next Sunday. After the service, Scott broke down and cried. He got down on his knees and asked for forgiveness. Colleen and Scott took our Starting Point Class together and began the process of finding faith in God and restoring their broken relationship. As the grace of Jesus poured into their individual lives, they learned to pour forth grace toward one another. Scott was baptized within weeks, and Colleen watched, wondering if she could trust the profound change she witnessed in her husband.

What gave Colleen great confidence was that Scott was engaging with a group of men in the church and was being mentored by a person she knew to be a straight shooter and a man of character and integrity. Scott was eating up the Scriptures and sharing what he was learning. He was becoming the man she had always dreamed of. During this process, Colleen asked their son, Connor, to come to service with them. He did, and he became involved in the young adult ministry. After a few months, Colleen and Connor professed Jesus as Lord and were baptized in the chilly waters off Maine's Pine Point.

During the summer, Colleen and Scott joined a marriage class that used Tim Keller's book, *The Meaning of Marriage*. They were so enthusiastic about practicing biblical principles of healthy relationships that the class leader asked them to assist in the sessions. Within a year, Colleen and Scott were co-leading the marriage ministry, and specializing in helping couples with relationship restoration.

It has been about seven years since Scott, Colleen, and Connor were baptized. They continue to lead within the marriage ministry, and Scott also serves as a men's ministry leader. Connor is engaged to a wonderful woman of God. In 2015, Colleen was diagnosed with colon cancer that had spread to her liver. Scott and Colleen have prayerfully walked through this challenge with the help of our Cancer Support Ministry. Their faithful obedience and hopeful spirit shine as powerful examples of God's transformative grace through Jesus Christ. The struggles and perseverance that Colleen and Scott have endured have produced profound faith and character. They are known for their compassion, patience, endurance, strength, wisdom, integrity, and fidelity in adversity.

10

And surely I am with you always

Matthew 28:20b

Wing Wong \\ Manchester, NH

A large group of Chinese from Mainland China crashed a peaceful and lawful pro-democracy demonstration rally of the "Hong Kongers" (as people from Hong Kong sometimes like to be referred) in front of the Massachusetts State House in Boston on August 18, 2019. They pushed themselves to the center stage of the rally holding up two huge Chinese flags and led the anti-protesters in yelling at the Hong Kongers with curses and hateful language. Poster boards were knocked down and stepped on, and one or two demonstrators were pushed to the ground when they marched through the city. To fight back, the Hong Kongers chanted, "Free Hong Kong! Protect Hong Kong! One China, two systems!" The rally was organized by the Hong Kong students in Boston to support the freedom of their fellow Hong Kongers across the ocean and to raise awareness among Bostonians to the critical situation happening in Hong Kong. I observed that there were many young people on both sides. One side was fighting to protect the human rights and humanitarian values that Hong Kong has enjoyed for two centuries, and the other side were people from Mainland China, trying to silence the Hong Kongers and treating them like their worst enemies. When seeing this, my heart sank and I asked, "Lord, how can I evangelize these young men and women from China?"

Doubtlessly, the disciples must have felt that it was impossible when Jesus told them to make disciples of all nations. How could they? They could not even persuade the Jews in Jerusalem to be followers of Jesus. Instead, the Jews crucified Jesus and chased after the disciples as criminals. On top of that, the One they relied on for direction, strength, and hope was going to leave them in a matter of minutes. Who could they rely on to tackle the evil and hostile world with the message of love and salvation? The answer was: "And surely I am with you always" (Matthew 28:20).

Without God, we can do nothing. When the Lord called me in 1970 to come to America in preparation to make disciples among the Chinese, I was hesitant. Finally, after the Lord strengthened my faith by revealing His will to me, I surrendered and stepped on the path that He had paved for me. With $25 in my pocket and some broken English, I started my journey on a jumbo jet to America. The Chinese used to say, "No money, no talk." I certainly had no money and even if I talked, people couldn't understand me. The Lord made what seemed impossible, possible. I had very little help from people. In fact, no missionaries in Hong Kong offered me any help. I can't recall if I received any letters from them when I was in Bible college. However, the Lord was always by my side, even when I was headstrong. He nurtured me and provided for me. Over the past 45 years, I have been able to start various disciple-making programs like radio broadcasting, Bible training institutions, correspondence courses, satellite classrooms in China, and have produced printed materials to help with disciple making. Our ministry started in Hong Kong and then spread to ten provinces in China with a core team of 12 people serving over 60 church leaders and hundreds of churches. God had made this timid and shy little boy become His servant-leader. Surely, without God, we can do nothing.

Praise the Lord, for He arms us with His promise and assurance when He sends us out to win the world for Him! Between the greatest historical event of all time — His Resurrection — and the greatest commission ever of making disciples of all nations, was the greatest proclamation: "All authority in heaven and on earth has been given to me" (Matthew 28:18). After Jesus discharged His command to His disciples, He closed with the greatest promise ever, "And surely I am with you always . . ." (Mathew 28:20).

When we engage ourselves in the Great Commission, we have the greatest partnership in the universe. Jesus assured us with certainty of His part in this by saying, "And surely I am with you always," right after He commanded His disciples to make disciples of all nations. I am sure you agree with me that there is no other partner greater than Jesus, for He is the Almighty God and nothing is impossible with Him. When the disciples heard how difficult it was for the rich to enter the Kingdom of God, they asked, "Who then can be saved?" Matthew recorded, "Jesus looked at them and said, 'With man this is impossible, but with God all things are possible.'" (Matthew 19:25–26).

A couple of years ago, I went back to a small town in Inner Mongolia where I had not visited for almost ten years. My co-worker in that region took me to a church building that they built after my last visit. We were then greeted by a group of church leaders. To my surprise, a 50-year-old brother came to me with a broad smile and asked, "Do you remember me?" I responded with a smile and apology, for I had no clue who he was. He told me when I had come to tell them about Jesus the last time, he yelled to my face that he would not believe in Jesus unless He would send rain to water their land because they had been in a drought for two years. He remembered that I had prayed for them on that specific request, and right after I left, God sent the rain. He was in awe and gave his life completely to God. He told me that his whole family became Christians, and that he had served in the church as a preaching deacon for about two years. Praise God that He is such a powerful partner! What seemed to be impossible, He made possible!

Jesus is also our most loving and caring partner. Matthew told us when Jesus saw the crowds, He had compassion on them because they were harassed and helpless, like sheep without a shepherd, so He had the disciples pray and sent them out to help these people (Matthew 9:36-10:1). Matthew portrayed Jesus as the compassionate God. He healed the sick, gave sight to the blind, fed the hungry, and raised the dead; but what struck me most was when He reached out His hand to touch the leper (Matthew 8:3). The Jews considered leprosy unclean both physically and spiritually. But Jesus touched him!

Have you ever met a leper? One early summer, the Lord sent me to Calcutta, India, to preach and teach for two months. I was stuck in traffic in a hot car even with all the windows down. All of a sudden, a filthy, blood-stained, and deformed hand with missing fingers and bad odor came through the window with palms stretched flat right in front of my face. My gosh! Leprosy! I was startled. I reached deep into my pocket to grab whatever rupees I had, and I put it all into that hand. I sighed a breath of relief as that hand quickly withdrew from the car! I was able to breathe again! And I rolled up all the windows right away. No, I never saw the face. In fact, his hand was all I saw. That was almost 40 years ago, yet I feel ashamed to this day. What a lesson to learn! Without Christ-like compassion, we will not be able to make disciples of all nations. After that, the Lord sent me to many poor and backward villages in China to make disciples for Him. There, they knew that I loved them and cared for them as Jesus loves and cares for me. If we honestly look into our own lives, we are no better than the lepers. Without Jesus' love and caring, we would be lost, like sheep without a shepherd. Praise God that we have such a loving and caring shepherd!

Jesus is also our faithful partner. Like a good shepherd, He faithfully watches over us and gives us the best care at all times. He said, "And surely I am with you always!" Sister Zhang was my student and core ministry team member in Inner Mongolia. It took her more than eight years to train and build up a team to make disciples throughout Inner Mongolia, and sometimes even cross over into Mongolia. When the church she started grew to more than 300 Christians, government authorities came and pressured them to turn the church over to government control. After two years of fighting back and forth with the government, the church elders and Christian leaders decided to submit to the government so they could preserve their building and receive financial aid from them. However, they had to stringently follow government policies, accept their leadership, preach and teach within their regulations, and not make disciples of all nations. This happened when Sister Zhang had gone on a mission trip to the Big Desert. It shattered Sister Zhang's heart when she returned, for none of the disciples she had trained remained with her. On top of that, her father was seriously hurt in a car accident. She felt so lonely, lost, and fragile, with no passion to continue on.

I wondered how Jesus might have felt when all His disciples deserted Him and fled when He was betrayed and arrested in the garden of Gethsemane (Matthew 26:56). Men for whom He had poured out His life over the past three years left at the time He needed them most. "Couldn't you men keep watch with me for one hour?" (Matthew 26:40b) was a desolate cry from a lonely soul. However, Jesus did not leave *them*. In fact, He died on the Cross and rose from the dead so He would be with them forever. Matthew highlighted Peter as an example. His denial of Jesus was another form of betrayal. Jesus' prediction of his betrayal served as a call to repentance and a sign of God's presence. Matthew wrote, "Then Peter remembered the word Jesus had spoken: 'Before the rooster crows, you will disown me three times.' And he went outside and wept bitterly" (Matthew 26:75).

Yes, unlike us, Jesus is a faithful partner. He will never forsake us, even when we push Him aside. Jesus knows exactly what we need to call us back to Him. In the lowest point of Sister Zhang's life, Jesus came to her rescue. One night, in her dream, she saw a picture that I had given her eight or nine years ago. Right away, she dug deep into her files and found the picture. It was a drawing of Jesus' hand holding someone's hand. She broke down in tears staring at the picture. All of a sudden, she realized Jesus was telling her that He was holding her hand all the time through the most disappointing and difficult journey of her life. Jesus had never left her. Images of God's constant love in her life kept flowing back into her memory. She got up as a new person the next day and started recruiting and making disciples for our Lord Jesus Christ. Praise the Lord, for Jesus always appears to us at the right time and in the right place to lead us through the valley of death and put us back on the mountain top again! Jesus is truly our most faithful and ready partner.

Matthew told us that the two Marys were filled with despair and sorrow when they could not find the body of Jesus in the tomb. What should they do? Suddenly, an angel appeared.

> The angel said to the women, "Do not be afraid, for I know that you are looking for Jesus, who was crucified. He is not here; he has risen, just as he said. Come and see the place where he lay. Then go quickly and tell his disciples: 'He has risen from the dead and is going ahead of you into Galilee. There you will see him.' Now I have told you." So the women hurried away from the tomb, afraid yet filled with joy, and ran to tell his disciples" (Matthew 28:5–8).

All of a sudden, Jesus met them and confirmed to them what the angel had just said (Matthew 28:9–10). These women came with tears and wandered with fear, but they left with joy because Jesus came to them at the right time and in the right place! Oh, as we go out into the world to make disciples for our Lord Jesus Christ, we are "like sheep among wolves" (Matthew 10:16a). We will meet with opposition and many obstacles, but we have the greatest partner. He is our Almighty God — loving, caring, faithful, and ready to help. Matthew gave us a great reminder from Jesus words:

> "Come to me, all you who are weary and burdened, and I will give you rest. Take my yoke upon you and learn from me, for I am gentle and humble in heart, and you will find rest for your souls. For my yoke is easy and my burden is light" (Matthew 11:28–30).

We used to sing this old hymn in church a lot: "What a fellowship, what a joy divine, leaning on the everlasting arms!" I wonder how many of us are truly aware of the meaning of this hymn. Matthew started his Gospel with "God came to us" (Matthew 1:1, 16, 20–21) and "God with us" (Matthew 1:23b), and ended with "God is with us" (Matthew 28:20b). This theme weaves through his Gospel from the beginning to the end. In one of our Chinese Sunday school class discussions, people shared different blessings that God had showered upon them: "Our son has found a job!" "Good health!" "Living in New Hampshire, quiet and no pollution!" "Freedom!" Well, it seemed I spoiled the fun when I raised this question: "If everything going good is considered a blessing, then why did the Apostle Peter tell us to rejoice in trials and sufferings?" (1 Peter 4:12-13). There was a long, silent pause. Everyone in the room seemed to be surprised by my question. Then I told them the greatest blessing that God had given us is "God with us." It is true that not many people consider "God with us" as a blessing greater than "a million dollars," "a healthy and beautiful body," or "a big house with no mortgage." But most of the things that people consider good may not give us full contentment and security. Only God can. When God is with us, our lives are filled with abundant love, joy, and peace, even in the most difficult circumstances. You see, we are not just Jesus' mission partners, we are also His friends and His brothers/sisters. We have a deep personal relationship with Jesus.

Before I wrote this paragraph today, I had just shared the gospel with a couple. One thing that I stressed to them is the lasting relationship we have with each other in heaven. This unique relationship is based on our lasting relationship with Jesus. When Jesus told His disciples that He is with them always, He did not indicate that it was merely a business partnership. "I am with you" is a personal relationship. Unlike a business partnership, our relationship will not be broken, even when the business is over or failed. "I am" is a current and continuous mode. Our relationship with Jesus is sealed by God. Nothing will take it away, even death. It is a lasting relationship. We can be full of hope when we look into the future because we have a lasting relationship with Jesus. Based on our relationship with Jesus, we can regard death as a relief from our physical boundary and look forward to the great reunion day with Jesus and all who believe in Him. Jesus promised His disciples a greater fellowship, according to Matthew. "I tell you, I will not drink from this fruit of the vine from now on until that day when I drink it new with you in my Father's kingdom" (Matthew 26:29).

Another blessing that comes with our personal relationship with Jesus is courage and confidence because of His faithfulness. We can put all our trust in Jesus because He is most faithful. Doesn't it seem odd to you that when Jesus sent the disciples to the Jews, He told them not to take any extra things with them including money, bag, cloak, sandals, or staff? Yet He said to them that He sent them out as sheep among wolves. He knew the danger but told His disciples that there was no need to over-prepare for it. Why? All I can think of is that Jesus wants us to wholly trust in Him to do His job His way. "But when they arrest you, do not worry about what to say or how to say it. At that time you will be given what to say, for it will not be you speaking, but the Spirit of your Father speaking through you" (Matthew 10:19–20). So, what's your excuse for not going and making disciples?

This same thing happened on one of our mission trips in Inner Mongolia. One night, the police came crashing into our humble lodging and arrested half of our team, including my son and me. They put us in separate rooms at the police station to be interrogated by a policeman and a National Security Bureau agent. After they took my son to another room, I told the policeman that my son looked Chinese but that he spoke no Mandarin Chinese because he was born and raised in America. So the policeman went to check on him. After a few minutes, he came back and scolded me for lying to him. He said my son understood and spoke Mandarin with no problem at all. I was surprised and puzzled. Was my son dating a Mandarin-speaking Chinese girl without me knowing it? Later, my son told me that somehow he was able to understand what they said and communicate with them using what he thought would sound like Mandarin. Well, I wish I could say that about my English. Yes, "your Father speaking through you" (Matthew 10:20b). Again, what's your excuse for not making disciples?

Fear? Yes. No sheep in its right mind goes into a den of wolves without fear. It is understandable and acceptable that we have fear. There's nothing wrong with that. However, we still go. Why? We go, not just because we know our God is powerful and faithful, but also because of love. Our loving relationship with Jesus surpasses all fears and concerns. May I remind you that you have to love Jesus more than yourself before you can be a follower of Jesus? In the Bible a young man wanted to follow Jesus. Jesus said to him, "Foxes have dens and birds have nests, but the Son of Man has no place to lay His head" (Matthew 8:20). He told the rich young ruler, "If you want to be perfect, go, sell your possessions and give to the poor, and you will have treasure in heaven. Then come, follow me" (Matthew 19:21). He said to His disciples, "Whoever wants to be my disciple must deny themselves and take up their cross and follow me" (Matthew 16:24). It sounds harsh, but not if you are deeply and truly in love. In fact, that was what Jesus did for us. He gave Himself up for us. He humbled and lowered Himself as the Son of Man, bore the shame, the pain, and was nailed on the Cross for us. However, His love does not end at the Cross. He loves us still. Jesus knows it is difficult and dangerous when we go to make disciples. We may be rejected, insulted, and persecuted. However, Jesus is always ready to wipe our sweat and tears away. He wraps us up in His arms and whispers, "Well done, my good and faithful servant" (Matthew 25:23). "And surely I am with you always" (Matthew 28:20). Praise God! Yes, "Blessed are you when people insult you, persecute you and falsely say all kinds of evil against you because of me [Jesus]. Rejoice and be glad, because great is your reward in heaven, for in the same way they persecuted the prophets who were before you" (Matthew 5:11–12). The turmoil of our labor turns into peace and joy because Jesus loves us!

However, we need to be reminded time and again that we have a powerful God who loves us all the time, wherever we are. Maybe the disciples were somewhat afraid, not knowing what to expect or what to do to make disciples of all nations. Jesus used the word ιδου right after He charged His disciples with the Great Commission to assure them of His presence. This word can be translated as "look" with an exclamation mark. It is a prompter of attention to arouse the audience to pay attention to what follows. It's a wake-up call from the Lord when we are captivated by fear. We need to pull our thoughts away from intimidating circumstances and put our focus back on the all-powerful and loving God who promised to never leave or forsake us.

We used to have a training center in a village in Guangzhou, China. Every other month or so, we brought the church leaders from different provinces in China to our two-week intensive training. After the two weeks, they would be sent home to practice what they had learned in their churches and come back for more training two months later. During the training, they had to stay inside our three-story training center to avoid any police suspicions or neighborhood watchdogs. One late night, our students were awakened by lots of noise, mixed with barking, meowing, and yelling. The village was lit up with vehicle headlights and search lights. Soon, they realized that the village was surrounded by police. They heard the police knocking at the neighbors' doors and yelling at people. Children were crying. Some people were pleading for mercy. It was chaotic. The police were making a surprise raid in the village. What should we do? What if the police came to our door? What if they saw our classroom and library full of Bibles and Bible study books? What if they found out that none of us registered with the local police station for staying in the village? What if . . . ? They were overwhelmed by fears. All of a sudden, someone remembered the memory verses that I gave them that morning:

> "Be strong and very courageous. Be careful to obey all the law my servant Moses gave you; do not

turn from it to the right or to the left, that you may be successful wherever you go. Keep this Book of the Law always on your lips; meditate on it day and night, so that you may be careful to do everything written in it. Then you will be prosperous and successful. Have I not commanded you? Be strong and courageous. Do not be afraid; do not be discouraged, for the LORD your God will be with you wherever you go" (Joshua 1:7–9).

This passage of Scripture was the prompter of attention planted by Jesus into their head earlier that morning. They knew there was nothing they could do to escape the police raid, but to trust God for deliverance. Jesus said, "Look!" This is the time to focus on Jesus rather than the threats. They all joined on their knees in a big circle before the Lord in the dark, holding onto God's promise of His presence. They recited the Scripture passage together softly from memory and prayed. After several prayers, they recited the Scriptures again. This went on in cycles all night. First, their prayers were full of urgent pleas. Then, some started to thank God for watching over them in the past. The last hour of their prayers were full of thanksgiving, praises, and hope! Somehow fears turned into peace, and tears turned into joy when they turned their focus from the threatening situation to God in prayer.

No one had watched the clock or paid attention to the raid any more. After many Amens, suddenly they realized that the police were gone and the village was quiet again. Of course, more praises went up to the Lord and they had a good nap after a restless night. I asked our campus manager to check with the neighbors mid-morning. He reported that all of their houses were searched by the police and several people were arrested for various reasons. Somehow, the police missed our door! Praise the Lord for keeping us safe! Surely, Jesus was with us!

I don't know if you've ever been in a very difficult situation where you felt you had no way out. However, all of a sudden, you realized you were not alone because Jesus was right there with you. The fear was gone. You were filled with peace, confidence, and joy. However, Jesus is not only with us at times of urgency, He is with us all the time. The problem is, we tend to forget about His presence when we are sailing in calm waters. Matthew told us that Jesus took the disciples on a boat trip and they sailed into a huge storm. The disciples, though some were fishermen, became scared, for they thought they would drown. But Jesus was peacefully sleeping. They went to wake Him up and said, "Lord, save us! We're going to drown!" (Matthew 8:25). Mark added this in his Gospel: "Teacher, don't you care if we drown?" (Mark 4:38b). What a false accusation and doubt of Jesus! Certainly Jesus cares. He is with us in both good and bad times.

Let's not forget that Jesus is not only with us on the outside, but inside of us as well. John the Baptist made this statement about Jesus, "I baptize you with water for repentance. But after me comes one who is more powerful than I, whose sandals I am not worthy to carry. He will baptize you with the Holy Spirit and with fire" (Matthew 3:11). The baptism of the Holy Spirit is God in us! This first happened on the day of Pentecost. Peter proclaimed the good news to the people and closed his address with a command and a promise, "Repent and be baptized, every one of you, in the name of Jesus Christ for the forgiveness of your sins. And you will receive the gift of the Holy Spirit. The promise is for you and your children and for all who are far off — for all whom the Lord God will call" (Acts 2:38–39). Now as Christians, "(We) have been crucified with Christ and (we) no longer live, but Christ lives in (us)" (Galatians 2:20). Our bodies became the temples of the Holy Spirit (1 Corinthians 6:18). "God with us" became "God in us"!

One day, I baptized over 80 people in a desert. My arms and back were getting sore but my heart was overflowing with joy. It had been our practice that after baptism we would have communion together. That afternoon, we all gathered outdoors on dry and sandy ground for the communion service. Many people were kneeling on the sand and stones. It was hot and dry. As I was giving thanks when we broke bread, a gust of wind suddenly blew through. It seemed our Lord Jesus smiled at us and told us that He had just given the Holy Spirit to all these new babes in Christ. You see, there had not been any breeze for the whole day until then. The word "wind" is the same as "spirit" in Greek. How blessed are we that Jesus comes to live in us when we accept Him as our Lord and Savior! We become one with Jesus! This is an indescribable blessing. It's not just beyond words but beyond our imagination. We are one with the King of kings and Lord of lords. We are one with the truth, light, and love. We are one with the Bread of Life. We are one with the Son of God. Then Jesus said, "Therefore go and make disciples of all nations, baptizing them in the name of the Father and of the Son and of the Holy Spirit, and teaching them to obey everything I have commanded you. And surely I am with you always, to the very end of the age" (Matthew 28:19–20). Amen.

Addendum

Queenie was exposed to Christianity while attending school in London. Her host family brought her to church and shared their Christian faith with her. After she came to New Hampshire, she was baptized into the Lord at Manchester Chinese Christian Church in 2010. She was hungry for the Word and a deeper relationship with Jesus. However, the church was not able to satisfy her need. She even went to Massachusetts for a four-day training class, but it did little good for her growth in Christ. Somehow, about the same time, the Lord moved me to start a discipleship program in the church. She became a committed student in my discipleship class. From there, she learned how to study the Bible on her own and grew in the Lord. She also learned to love and serve through teaching our children's Sunday school and leading the Chinese outreach fellowship and campus group activities. We met almost every week and shared not only the Bible, but also our personal lives. She started working for our ministry part-time in January 2016, and in July 2019 she became our full-time partner and started picking up some leadership responsibilities that help us to make disciples for our Lord Jesus Christ.

11

To the very end of the age

Matthew 28:20c

Brian Mowrey \\ Bethel, CT

I used to think I had all the time in the world, but now I know that every moment is precious. Growing up in New England, I always loved the winters. Sledding down dangerously steep hills, building igloos, and having snowball fights with my friends still bring great memories to mind. Winter was fun, but summer was the best, mainly because my birthday is in July. As a kid, birthdays couldn't come fast enough. My mom kept a calendar hanging near our rotary phone. (She still does.) When the page got turned from June to July, I could see the big red circle around the number 27. I was so excited it was July, but it seemed like an impossible amount of time before my birthday would arrive. Twenty-seven days was like eternity to an impatient elementary-aged kid. I thought the red-circled day would never arrive. If I could have, I would have skipped the uncircled days altogether. As a kid, I couldn't speed up time fast enough, and now I'm desperately trying to slow it down. Once I tried to race past every moment to get to the moment I was waiting for, but now I've learned that every moment is precious and valuable. Each moment is an opportunity to walk with the Lord and step into great opportunities serving and following Jesus.

Jesus has a day circled in red as well, but we can't see His calendar. He alone knows the date and time. The temptation is to try and fast forward to the red-circled day and skip all the others. We long for the day when Jesus will return and put all things back to right; however, the day has not yet arrived. So how are we to live until that day? The words of Jesus in Matthew 28:16–20 instruct us to live well in the days leading up to His long-awaited return. The day is coming when we will be with Him, and all pain and suffering will cease, but until then we have been given a great and worthy mission, and this mission lasts "to the very end of the age."

The last seven words of Jesus in the Gospel of Matthew are about commitment. When Jesus says, "to the very end of the age" (Matthew 28:20), He is expressing His commitment to us as His followers, as well as communicating the extent of His call and command on our lives to go and make disciples. Jesus is assuring us as His disciples that He will always be with us as we serve Him leading up to the great red-circled day. He is also compelling us to keep going. The mission to make disciples is not done until Jesus returns. This call on our lives should not turn on and turn off. It's a part of who we are until Jesus returns. He is unfailingly and unconditionally committed to us, and we are to be unwaveringly committed to His call on our lives to make disciples.

Our church hosts a Family Fair around Halloween each year. The idea is to have a safe place for families to dress up and have fun, and to open the doors of the church to the community. There are prizes, games, bounce houses, and face painting. It's a ton of fun. One particular year, there was even a prize for the best group costume. My four daughters decided to dress up as the minions. You know, the little yellow guys from the Minions movies. To make the experience more accurate, they asked me to dress up as Gru, their leader. One of Gru's most prominent features is that he is bald. Hoping to win the group prize, my girls asked . . . correction . . . demanded that I shave my head. I said no. One of my daughters said, "I mean, come on, Papa, how committed are you to this?" To which the answer was, "Not very." This is the question on the table right now, as you finish up this book of sermons Matthew 28:16–20. How committed are you to this? Jesus is not asking you to surrender your hair (if you still have some); His request is much bigger. He's asking you to surrender your life to Him and His call to lead others into deeper relationship with Him. It's the greatest mission. It's not the easiest, but it is certainly the most fulfilling. And it requires commitment "to the very end of the age."

In Jesus we have a great example of what it is to be committed to discipling others. The life of Jesus gives us a perfect picture of what it looks like to walk with others as they learn and grow in their walk with the Lord. Four lessons about commitment come to mind as we heed the call to make disciples "to the very end of the age."

Lesson Number 1: Commitment Is Not a Problem for Jesus

The year was 1932 and the New York Yankees were playing against the Chicago Cubs in the World Series. It was game three and the score was tied four to four in the ninth inning when the Yankee's greatest slugger came to the plate — Babe Ruth. The Great Bambino, the Sultan of Swat, the Caliph of Clout watched strike one pass by without swinging the bat. Just before the second pitch, he would do something no one had ever done before and no one has done since. He picked up his bat and pointed to the center field fence. Call it prophetic, call it arrogant, but he was calling his shot. In Babe Ruth fashion, he was confidently predicting a home run to center field. The second pitch was delivered. Strike two. He raised his bat and pointed over the center field fence for a second time. The third pitch was delivered. Crack! Ruth swung, struck the ball, and then watched it soar over the very spot his foretelling motion had just predicted. The Yankees won the game, and the legend that was Babe Ruth grew.

Now, if Ruth had struck out, we wouldn't be talking about this story. We would be talking about Lou Gehrig, who like Ruth, hit a home run the very next at-bat. It's not much of a story if someone claimed to hit a home run and then struck out. It's only a great story because he made a commitment and followed through. Do you know that Jesus pointed to something as well? It wasn't a home run — it was an empty tomb. He pointed to the fact that He would rise from the dead, and He fulfilled that commitment. Matthew 16:21 serves as a turning point. "From that time on Jesus began to explain to his disciples that he must go to Jerusalem and suffer many things at the hands of the elders, the chief priests and the teachers of the law, and that he must be killed and on the third day be raised to life." These were Jesus' commitments and He would fulfill each one. Jesus does not have a problem with commitment. When He makes a promise, He fulfills that promise.

When we arrive at Matthew 28:16–20, we can be assured that Jesus will fulfill the promises that He has made because Jesus does not have a problem with commitment. Jesus tells us that all authority has been given to Him. We have no reason to doubt that our Jesus is fully credentialed and perfectly able to call upon heaven as we go and make disciples of all nations. His call on our life is directly connected to His commitment to being the authority of God in and through us as we make disciples. We can trust this commitment.

In the same manner, we can fully trust His commitment to be with us — always. Jesus never failed His disciples with His presence. He was with them when everyone was hungry (Matthew 14), when storms raged (Matthew 14), when they got it right and when they got it wrong (Matthew 16:13–23), and even when they fell asleep (Matthew 26:40). His commitment to be with them was unwavering. We can trust in the fact that Jesus has never failed to be present with His disciples; therefore, He will never fail to be present with each of us as we follow Him. In fact, He ascended to heaven so that He could fulfill this commitment to all people by sending His promised Holy Spirit — His very presence through the power of His Spirit within all who believe.

Lesson Number 2: Commitment Determines Direction

I love the story in the Bible of Ruth. It's a beautiful story about the sacrifice, challenge, and blessing of commitment. After a series of major losses, Ruth decides to remain committed to her mother-in-law, Naomi, even though it would mean turning from her hometown and stepping into a new life. Her commitment to Naomi determined her direction. She could have easily turned back to her hometown, Moab, but she had a new commitment that guided her life.

We have the chance to turn back to Moab as well — back to an old life. Old friendships come back into the equation, trying to pull us back into an old life. Old addictions taunt us and tease us. Old relationships knock on the door. Old patterns of life gradually try to sneak back in. Old fears begin to control us once again. And we have a choice. Will we return to Moab, or like Ruth, will we turn to Jesus and say, "Where you go I will go" (Ruth 1:16)? For Ruth, her commitment determined her direction.

Surrendering your life to Jesus changes everything. Following Jesus does not mean that we take our already established lives and just put Jesus in wherever He fits. If you want to follow Jesus as a disciple and as one who disciples, it's all or nothing. He is either the Lord of your life or not.

There is a great story in 1 Kings chapter 17. Elijah the prophet has just delivered a harsh word to King Ahab. As you can imagine, Elijah no longer feels safe around the king. Luckily God gives Elijah directions. He commands Elijah to go eastward and hide in a ravine. Then the Lord makes a promise. He tells Elijah that He will provide water for him there and the ravens would supply him with food. To me this sounds a bit unconventional. I've heard of Uber-eats, but ravens delivering food? I'm just not sure. I love what happens next. Scripture simply says, "So he did" (1 Kings 17:5). Why did Elijah do exactly what the Lord commanded? It wasn't because it all made sense to him. He did it because of his commitment to the Lord, and his commitment determined his direction.

To be called a disciple means that we will follow the call and commands of God. It can be natural to return to Moab and go back to what is comfortable, but discipleship means wholeheartedly following the Lord no matter the cost. How is Moab knocking on your door right now? Will you answer the door, or will you allow your commitment to Jesus to determine your direction? As you disciple others, will you encourage them and point them into their new life, directed by their commitment to Jesus?

Lesson Number 3: Commitment Always Overrules Comfort

Resisting the temptation of Satan must not have been comfortable (Matthew 4). It wasn't comfortable for Jesus when He was rejected in His hometown (Matthew 13). I'm sure it wasn't comfortable for Jesus to have to defend Himself against the Pharisees (Matthew 19). It certainly wasn't comfortable for Jesus on the Cross (Matthew 27). Yet His commitment led Him into each of these situations. If Jesus had judged His decisions based on comfort, He would have never completed the mission for which He came. His commitment was to destroy the work of the evil one and set the captives free. Through His commitment to be the final sacrifice, He has invited all to be saved. Was it always comfortable? No, not even close. Was it fruitful? Beyond what we can even imagine.

My friend, John, was walking through his house one day and he noticed a sign hung on his teenage son's door that read, "No Trespassing, Keep Out!" I don't need to tell you how that went over, but it did get me thinking. How often do I put up a "No Trespassing, Keep Out!" sign in one of the rooms of my life? How often do I shut Jesus out because I don't want Him to come in and see what is really going on? On another occasion, my wife and I were given concert badges that read, "VIP All Access." This is the sign the Lord is looking for His disciples to hang on their hearts. Have complete and full access in my life, Lord, "to the very end of the age." Nothing is off limits. Nothing is hidden. Will this lead to some discomfort? Yes. However, it's the life that leads to the greatest adventures with the Lord. It's the life of a disciple. When it comes to our lives as disciples, there should not be a room that is closed off to the Lord. He wants all of us because He gave all of Himself for us.

Until commitment overrules comfort, the renewal and re-vival that we long to see will remain a dream instead of a reality. Comfort leads to a slumbering faith, whereas commitment leads to a contagious faith. When Jesus says, "to the very end of the age," He is calling us to persevere in a faith that He modeled for us — a committed faith that welcomes the invitations of Jesus and is bold enough to get uncomfortable. I think of Peter who received a vision from the Lord in Acts 10. The command was to go to Cornelius' house. Peter, a Jewish man, was called by God to step into the house of a Gentile. This was unheard of. Yet Peter says yes. He breaks the threshold of hundreds of years of division. He preaches the Gospel to a hungry people. Through this obedi-ence and willingness to be uncomfortable, the entire landscape of Christianity is changed forever. The Lord wants to change the landscape again. Are we ready to allow commitment to overrule comfort?

Lesson Number 4: Commitment Invites the Power of God

In Matthew 28:18, Jesus tells His disciples that He has been giv-en "all authority in heaven and on earth." Nothing is out of the reach of Jesus. He can do "immeasurably more than all we ask or imagine" (Ephesians 3:20). I'm not a very good poker player — probably a good sign as a pastor. However, sometimes when I play cards with my family, I look at my hand and think I have nothing. Then I lay down my hand and discover, embarrassingly, that I could have won. Sometimes I forget about what I have in my hand. This is so true in my spiritual life as well. Sometimes I forget what I carry around every day. Friends, we are empowered by the Spirit of God. This is the Spirit of Jesus, who has made His home within us. This is the same Jesus who has been given all authority in heaven and earth. We do not go about our mission empty-handed.

When I was in college, I was in a band. (Don't look it up. We weren't very good.) On one of our trips, we found ourselves in Montana playing at a youth conference. We stayed at a friend's house. Mr. Joe was a pastor and a rancher, which I discovered is the case for nearly every person in Montana. Everyone has a job, and they also work on a ranch, or so it seems. Mr. Joe told us he needed our help one day. He had a great mission for us. He needed us to help him get the cattle from one pasture to a smaller pen. He put me in charge of the gate at the smaller pen, telling me to open it when the cattle came down the hill and close it once all the cattle were in the pen. He also told me I would need to direct the cattle into the pen. For this task, he gave me a tennis racket. Mind you, I have no experience as a rancher. Then Mr. Joe got on his four-wheeler. I said, "Hey, where are you going?"

He replied, "I'm going to encourage the cows in this direction. All you have to do is point them into the pen."

I said, "All I have is this tennis racket."

He said, "You have everything you need; trust me." Sure enough, the cattle came down the hill and I directed them into the pen with my Wilson tennis racket. I thought I was ill-equipped, but the rancher knew I had everything I needed. God has given us a high calling — a great mission. And He gives us more than we need — something much better than an old tennis racket. He gives us the gift of His Spirit.

Our only task is to remain committed to the Lord. When the Lord calls us, it's through our commitment to Him that the power of God is invited into the situation. If we want to see the power of God, we need to commit and devote our lives to Him. The power of God comes through radical obedience. 2 Chronicles 16:9 says, "For the eyes of the LORD range throughout the earth to strengthen those whose hearts are fully committed to him." Once found, the Lord empowers the committed to usher in His Kingdom through His power. As His disciple, what is God asking of you? Will you say "yes"? I believe your "yes" will be the invitation the Lord is looking for to move powerfully in and through you. There is nothing more exciting.

How Committed Are You?

Simen Krueger is a cross-country skier from Norway. In the 2018 Winter Olympics, he was competing in the 30km race. At the very beginning of the race, Krueger crashed into a few other skiers and found himself at the back of the pack. Slowly but consistently, Krueger began climbing to the front, overtaking one skier at a time. Eventually, Krueger found himself in first place and never looked back. He was devoted and committed to winning. He never ruled himself out and kept his eyes on the thing that mattered most to him. It would have been easy to have become distracted by the crash, by the difficulty of overcoming it, yet he never gave up on the purpose of all his training and all his dedication. I wonder, am I that committed to Jesus? Are you? God is calling us to be all in — "to the very end of the age." These last seven words from Jesus challenge us to keep going, making the most of every moment as we follow Him as disciples and as we disciple others.

Jesus has drawn a red circle around a day that is coming. He will return. Our hearts groan in anticipation for that day. But let's also rejoice in the days in between where we can sow seeds into the Kingdom of God and lead people into a loving relationship with Jesus. Let's commit to the call of Jesus to "make disciples of all nations, baptizing them in the name of the Father and of the Son and of the Holy Spirit, and teaching them to obey everything I have commanded you" (Matthew 28:19–20). And let's remember that we don't go at this alone. He is with us always. And as we look to that red-circled day, let's make the most of our time by passionately and boldly sharing Jesus with others. How committed are you?

Addendum

It all started with a guitar. Matt is one of the most talented guys I know. He walked into the church one day carrying his guitar. Turns out, he was an excellent guitar player. I wasn't sure where he was in his faith at the time, but I would soon find out. One afternoon my family and I were eating at McDonalds. (Don't judge me.) While we were eating I saw several ambulances pull into the parking lot. I went out to see what had happened and to my disbelief I saw Matt lying on the ground. He had taken heroin and passed out. I met the family at the hospital and prayed as Matt slowly recovered. I told Matt that he had a choice: to try and overcome this addiction on his own, or with Jesus. He chose Jesus. For several years I met with Matt every other week. He committed himself to the Lord and sought help to overcome his addiction. As we met, we would pray together and talk together. I helped Matt discover his calling, and today I'm so happy to say that Matt serves as a Worship Pastor at a growing church. None of us are perfect. The question is, will we choose to walk alone or walk with Jesus? Matt chose Jesus. And I'm so glad he did.

12

The Priority of Discipleship

Matthew 28:16–20

Scott Gibson \\ South Hamilton, MA, and Waco, TX

Introduction

When you noted the biblical text on which I'll be speaking, some of you had a wide, open-mouthed yawn; that is, those of you who are acquainted with this familiar text. Those seated around you might not have seen the yawn, or even heard it. But you know what I mean. It's a text some of you have heard before — yawn — many times before.

But let's test the yawn-factor with a quiz. I like quizzes. When you hear the text address of Matthew 28:16–20, what do you typically think? What would you say this text is about?

Missions, right?

When we hear that the text of the sermon is Matthew 28:16–20, we think of going to foreign lands and being boiled in a pot of hot grease because of our commitment to Christ.

When we hear that the text of the sermon is Matthew 28:16–20, we envision going to the coldest of climates, like Antarctica, and eking out a meager existence for the gospel.

"There's a story to tell to the nations . . ." the old missions hymn pulsates in our chests and the words remind us of the call to go into all the world.

What if I were to tell you that the em-PHA-sis is in on the wrong syl-AB-ble? That going to the far-reaches of the earth is certainly part of what Jesus wants us to do, but there's more to what he's called us to do than go to the far corners of the globe?

That's what we want to do as we examine afresh Matthew 28:16–20. We want to turn to those words and ask the question, "What did Jesus instruct His disciples to do? What does He tell us to do as we work with Him to build his church?" As you read it again, try to hear it again for the very first time:

Matthew writes: "Then the eleven disciples went to Galilee, to the mountain where Jesus had told them to go. When they saw him, they worshiped him; but some doubted. Then Jesus came to them and said, 'All authority in heaven and on earth has been given to me. Therefore go and make disciples of all nations, baptizing them in the name of the Father and of the Son and of the Holy Spirit, and teaching them to obey everything I have commanded you. And surely I am with you always, to the very end of the age.' "

What is this text saying? What is it getting at? We might think of missions and evangelism.

We sometimes think that evangelism is all there is — that this is what the text is talking about.

This text is often used as an evangelism or "missions" text. Our little quiz we took moments ago demonstrates this. Preachers and missionaries have reinforced the interpretation of this text. The starting place for this understanding of the text is the desire of Jesus — at least in the English translation: "Therefore as you go. . . ."

That's where preachers and missions advocates usually stop. GO! That's what Jesus assumes we will do — go! Go into the neighborhood, go into the countryside, go into the urban centers of the world, go to the countries around the globe.

But more than that, the emphasis is on "making disciples." As you go, tell others about Jesus. As you go, tell men and women and boys and girls about Jesus so they can be saved from their sin. And as you go, evangelize.

"Go" is a good word. I like it. Evangelism is a good thing.

While in college, I was involved in campus ministry that focused on evangelism. As members of this group, we were required to make a certain number of contacts each week. That is, we were required to share the gospel with a set amount of folks weekly.

We also went on evangelistic visits to student apartments or dorm rooms with an experienced, older student in the campus ministry. Did everyone with whom we shared the good news of Jesus' love for them respond positively? No. But we, I trust, were used by God to plant a seed in their lives from which faith eventually would grow.

I'm really an introvert — I'm really a quiet type of person. The emphasis on going and evangelizing pushed me out of my comfort zone and taught me that I have something of incomparable value to share with others — salvation in Christ.

We may think that this biblical text is about going, about missions and evangelizing. The importance of spreading the good news of salvation in Jesus Christ is key to "going into all the world." And we may struggle with evangelizing — but we can't get away from the responsibility of doing it. And certainly, this biblical text implies its importance.

But what we see from this passage is something different.

Going is the route; discipleship is the goal.

"As you go." Jesus here states the primary emphasis of the text: "make disciples." Translations are a funny thing — they don't always pick up on the nuances, the various aspects of meaning in a passage. But what we discover in examining this text in the original language is that the words that dominate are "make disciples."

The disciples were to make more disciples. They were to evangelize. However, they were not to leave people at conversion, but move them to maturity in discipleship. To be a disciple means to be a learner — not just the teachings of Jesus (doctrine), but also the life and character of Jesus. Jesus' disciples were to instruct the teachings of Jesus and, through their lives, demonstrate the life and character of Jesus.

I understood the power of discipleship when I served as a pastor. One of the questions that concerned me as a pastor was why the people I was shepherding didn't know the Bible? Why is it that they don't know how to live and act in a Christian, civil manner with each other? Why is it that they don't use their money or time as if it were God's, not theirs? The answer is discipleship. To be a disciple means to be a learner. To be a disciple means that these folks are to know and live the teachings of Jesus.

We may find it difficult to get our brains wrapped around what I'm talking about. We live in a Christian culture that is heavily influenced by consumerism. People go to the store and buy what they want. People go to restaurants and eat what they want. Christians go to a certain church and don't like what they see or experience: The church is too small; the church is too big; the church doesn't offer what I want; the church doesn't have a full-service children's program; the sermons don't feed me; the preacher is too short; the preacher is too tall; the preacher is _____ (you fill in the blank); the church is _____ (you fill in the blank).

We've shaped following Jesus and being a disciple into our own image. Let me tell you something. Most of the time, we don't know what we really need — and very often, what we want isn't what we need. Discipleship is costly. Following Jesus is demanding. It is not cheap, quick, nor easy. Discipleship is for the long haul.

This text is mainly about discipleship.

There's no doubt about it, discipleship matters when it comes to growing the church.

The text says that some of the disciples of Jesus doubted. The disciples perhaps doubted on several levels when they saw Jesus and heard His command. They may have doubted that He really was alive. They may have doubted that they were up to carrying on the ministry He gave to them. They may have doubted that He would see them through His commission. But there was no doubt about this one: discipleship matters when it comes to growing the church.

Being a disciple, a learner of Jesus, is the road toward maturity. This means taking our salvation in Christ seriously.

Recently, I was working on a book about moving a congregation from one level of spiritual maturity to another. The book teaches how to assess where a congregation is, generally, on the scale of infant, toddler, child, adolescent, young adult, middle-aged adult, or senior adult. Each church is different. Some churches are more mature than others, while other churches are less mature than others. My challenge to pastors is to plan sermons that will help churches move from one level of spiritual maturity to the next. This means that listeners — like you — are called to take your salvation in Christ seriously. It means that you don't want to be spoon-fed your faith, but that you take an active role in being a learner, a disciple, because you want to mature.

What we discover is that maturity doesn't come easily. Sometimes we resist growing. We like it where we are. Because we've become accustomed to being a child in the faith, nothing too challenging can be expected of us. We're used to where we are as an adolescent. We can make excuses for how we behave, even if it's immaturely. Growth is tough — but this is what Jesus expects from us — and what we should expect from each other, especially if the church is going to grow and mature. There's no doubt about it, discipleship matters when it comes to growing the church.

Conclusion

If we want to grow numerically as a church, our first order of business is discipleship. It's grabbing hold of our commitment to Christ and helping each other to grow in faith by being committed to knowing and understanding God's Word, regularly worshiping with other disciples, engaging in a Bible reading plan, cultivating a habitual prayer life, and getting another disciple who is more mature in faith to mentor us.

You will not reach your full potential as a believer in Jesus Christ by only attending worship on Sundays. Let's face it, it's an hour out of the 168 hours in a week. Do you think that's enough time to be the mature believer you've been called to be? There's no doubt about it, discipleship matters when making disciples. Making disciples is the way Christ will build His church until the end of the age.

We're all in this together. The church is built on men and women deepening themselves in their faith, in what they believe, and in the making of more disciples. I'm absolutely convinced of this. I've seen it in the churches I've served and those where I've done consulting and have preached. There's no doubt about it, discipleship matters when it comes to changing the world where you live.

There's no doubt about it, discipleship matters when it comes to following Jesus.

Addendum

For almost 30 years I've served as a seminary professor, training hundreds of students to preach. However, what motivates me more than anything else is the privilege of mentoring — discipling — students. My approach is "No program but time, no book but the Bible." I meet with two or three students over the course of their three-year Master of Divinity degree program, looking to the Scriptures and shaping their lives according to it. Once a week, the student comes to our home and we share a meal together. Following the meal, the student and I study, talk, and pray together. But the relationship doesn't stop at graduation — it continues for years as we keep in touch regularly, as I preach at ordinations and conduct weddings. Discipleship — being a learner in Christ — doesn't stop for any of us until we're in the presence of the Lord. These men — and a few women — whom I've discipled mean more to me than I can express. They are my sons and daughters in the faith. To read more about them, see *No Program but Time, No Book but the Bible*, edited by Matthew D. Kim.

Appendix 1

Sermon Outlines

Then
(Matthew 28:16a)

Introduction
Personal Conversion Story
- Growing up in a non-religious home
- Angry alcoholic agnostic
- Best friend's drunk driving accident
- Invitation to church
- The church's influence in my conversion.

A Disciple-Making Church

- Church members discipled me in faith and life.
- The pastor mentored me in hermeneutics and homiletics.
- Preached my first sermon six months after I was saved.
- God used the church's discipleship to call me to pastoral ministry.
- Church obeyed the Great Commission

The Components of Discipleship (Matthew 28:16–20)

- The Imperative — Making disciples is the main component of the Great Commission.
- The Participles — The three components of discipleship.
  1. "Going" — building intentional relationships with the lost.
  2. "Baptizing" — a public profession of repentance and faith in Jesus Christ

3. "Teaching" — instruction in all facets of the Christian life.
- The Illustration — My little country church never grew numerically because it practiced the Great Commission so well.

The Call of Discipleship in the Gospel of Matthew

- Jesus practiced the Great Commission before he preached the Great Commission!

Calling the First Disciples (Matthew 4:18–22)

- Jesus met the fishermen on their turf and utilized their language when he called them to discipleship.

Calling of Matthew (Matthew 9:9–13)

- Jesus was willing to associate with uncouth characters for the sake of discipleship.

Sending Out the Twelve (Matthew 10)

- Jesus empowered and unleashed the Twelve disciples for ministry.

Conclusion

- Implementing the Great Commission in rural Vermont.

JASON MCCONNELL (Franklin, VT)

The eleven disciples went to Galilee, to the mountain where Jesus had told them to go (Matthew 28:16b)

Now the eleven disciples went to Galilee, to the mountain to which Jesus had told them to go (Matthew 28:16).

A. Who Is Judas?
- Ref. Matthew 27:3–10
- Judas undoubtedly spent countless hours with Jesus and witnessed His work up close, yet he was lured by 30

pieces of silver. He exchanged his position in Jesus' "inner circle" for worldly desires.

B. The Meeting at the Mountain at Galilee

- Ref. Matthew 17:1–9
- Many scholars have concluded that this mountain was the same one where Jesus was transfigured. When Jesus transformed into a more glorious, radiant, and beautiful state, as told in Matthew's Gospel.
- I want to be a follower of Christ because it grants me access to the meeting where I can experience the love and glory of Christ.

C. We Need Jesus

- Matthew 28:16 carries great significance. It issues us warning to put our trust in the Lord or be ousted from the promise of Christ. If our trust is not in Jesus, we are relying on human strength. We will spend our time searching for worldly validation rather than letting the gospel do the work.
- Jesus came and fulfilled a plan of success in spite of the world's destiny for disaster. But it's through the Gospel and God's great love that we are no longer separated but reunited with Christ.
- Present the gospel (i.e: This love is beautiful and so simple. It was Thursday that He ate His last supper. He went to the garden to pray but was arrested. He was tried and found guilty although He was innocent. But it was His mission to die for the guilty so that we could stand before the throne innocent. They beat Him, ripped His clothes, and put a crown of thorns on His head. They nailed Him to the Cross. They gave Him vinegar when He was thirsty and pierced Him in His side to ensure He was dead. While He hung on the Cross in agony, Jesus still showed love when He said, "Father, forgive them for

they know not what they do!" He died so that we can experience the greatest love.

MICHAEL BAILEY (Bloomfield, CT)

When they saw Him, they worshiped Him
(Matthew 28:17a)

Introduction: In this message, our focus will be three words from Matthew 28:17: "they worshiped him."

I. The Backstory:

    A.Matthew's account leading up to the Great Commission
    B.God put the need to worship inside us
        1. The thrill of victory
        2. The tragedy and victory of the Cross and Resurrection

II. What Is Worship?

A. Definition: Worship is a life-expression of praise and thanksgiving for who God is, what He has done, what He is doing, and what He will do

B. Second: Worship must be my/your whole life (Isaiah 1 — unacceptable worship)

C, First: Worship is focused on God (Romans 12:1 — acceptable worship)
        1. Praise and thanksgiving for who He is — Psalm 102:12
        2. Praise and thanksgiving for what He has done
        3. Praise and thanksgiving for what He is doing
        4. Praise and thanksgiving for what He will do —
            1 John 3:1–3.
        5. Revelation 4:8-11

"They Worshiped Him"

A. The emotional roller coaster of the Apostles in Galilee

B. Discipleship begins with a life of worship — Luke 14:27

Personal Examination

FRANK REYNOLDS (Candia, NH)

But some doubted
(Matthew 28:17b)

Introduction

Connect with the audience through a shared experience that when things often seem too good to be true, they often are too good to be true.

> Then the eleven disciples went to Galilee, to the mountain where Jesus had told them to go. When they saw him, they worshiped him; but some doubted. Then Jesus came to them and said, "All authority in heaven and on earth has been given to me. Therefore go and make disciples of all nations, baptizing them in the name of the Father and of the Son and of the Holy Spirit, and teaching them to obey everything I have commanded you. And surely I am with you always, to the very end of the age" (Matthew 28:16–20).

Feeling It

Introduce the text of doubt as a descriptor for the apostles on the mountain. Connect with the audience about how doubt is useful and even beneficial, not necessarily a bad thing.

> When they saw him, they worshiped him; but some doubted (Matthew 28:17).

Getting It

Our doubts are mostly rooted in the question of God's goodness, not God's existence. Bring in Matthew 14 and Peter walking on the water. Why could Peter jump out of the boat and sink all within a few steps? Faith helps us take many steps in our life, but doubting if God is there in the wind and the waves is where we need to realize that Jesus understands our suffering.

> Immediately Jesus reached out his hand and caught him [Peter]." You of little faith," he said, "why did you doubt?" (Matthew 14:31).

The Good News

Jesus experienced our suffering and understands our doubts. Jesus cried out, "My God, My God why have you forsaken me?" But Jesus did not die as every other sage, prophet, and reformer. Jesus rose from the dead. That is why the Apostles brought their doubts to the mountain that day. Where else would they go?

> About three in the afternoon Jesus cried out in a loud voice, *"Eli, Eli, lema sabachthani?"* (which means, "My God, my God, why have you forsaken me?") (Matthew 27:46).

Living It

The good news is that it only takes a mustard seed of faith. You don't have to be a saint, or super-religious, or a Bible scholar. Just enough faith in that moment of desperation is sufficient to reach out to God. God is good in the place where faith in nothing cannot be good. We do not do it alone. We do not climb that mountain with our doubts alone, we climb it with others. All it takes is the first step of confessing our need for God, in spite of our doubts, because God can pull us up even in the midst of our questions and doubts.

> Then the disciples came to Jesus in private and asked, "Why couldn't we drive it [demon] out? He replied, "Because you have so little faith. Truly I tell you, if you have faith as small as a mustard seed, you

can say to this mountain, 'Move from here to there' and it will move. Nothing will be impossible for you" (Matthew 17:19–21).

TIM HAWKINS (Boston, MA)

All authority in heaven and on earth has been given to me (Matthew 28:18)

Theme: Remember the authority of Jesus

Introduction

I. Why do we become discouraged?

    A. We are human.
    B. We feel God has let us down.
    C. We experience rejection.
    D. We take our eyes off God.

II. As we go

    A. He rules.
    B. He commands.
    C. He calls.
        1. To ministry
        2. To place

II. It goes with us.

    A. It goes before us.
    B. It goes in us.
    C. It goes after us.

DAVID SMITH (Nashua, NH)

Therefore go
(Matthew 28:19a)

I. Introduction
    A. The Commission Stated
    B. The Commission Confused
    C. The Commission Abandoned

II. What is the Mission?
    A. What is a True Disciple?
        1. Job Description method
        2. Jesus' method
    B. How Does a True Disciple Follow?
        1. The Vine and the Branches
            a. The Illustration Explained
            b. The Illustration Applied
            c. Remains (Abiding) Explained
            d. Remains (Abiding) Applied

III. What is Getting in the Way of True Discipleship?
    A. Our Failure to Make Disciples as We Go, Wherever We Go
    B. Our Part in Remaining (Abiding)
    C. Return to the Great Commission

RICK FRANCIS (Scarborough, ME)

Make disciples of all nations
(Matthew 28:19b)

Introduction: What is the Great Commission?
- A biblical mandate?
- Or 30%?

Great Commission — or Great Commissions?
- Beyond just Matthew 28:18–20
- Other post-Resurrection statements of Jesus that help us understand Matthew 28:18–20 and "make disciples of all nations"

- Matthew 28:18–20: go and make disciples of all nations
- Mark 16:15–18: ". . . into all the world and preach . . . to all creation"
- Luke 24:45–49: preached in His name to all nations, beginning at Jerusalem
- Acts 1:8: ". . . you will be my witnesses in Jerusalem, and in all Judea and Samaria, and to the ends of the earth"
- John 20:21–22: "As the Father has sent me, I am sending you"

Combine these statements, and the conclusion is unavoidable. Jesus wants to send us (John 20:21), His followers:
- To all nations (Matthew and Luke)
- To the entire creation (Mark)
- And to our homelands (Jerusalem), our regions (Judea), across cultures locally (Samaria), and cross culturally globally (ends of the earth) (Acts)

Remember how radical these words were to Jesus' Jewish, ethnocentric disciples: Jesus was taking them outside their comfort zone.

Matthew 28:16–20 – Sent Out with Superlatives

Our focus today, Matthew 28:19b, gives us a sense of not only the global nature of our mission as followers of Christ, but also the end result Jesus had in mind — making disciples. To enlarge our understanding of the mandate to "make disciples of all nations," it helps to realize that Matthew's Great Commission record builds on four superlatives:

1. Our platform for outreach: his supreme authority. "All authority" is His. Triumph over death is the power behind us.
2. The content of our proclamation: teaching others to obey ALL that He taught. Discipleship, not "Christianity light."
3. The destination of our outreach — ALL nations (or all ethnic groups). His superlative vision is for all the peoples on earth.

4. A superlative promise — "I am with you ALWAYS." In other words, Jesus says, "There's no place you can go that I won't go with you. I'll give you the words to speak and the love to share. I'll be the one empowering your words, and I'm the one who can break through to enlighten peoples' hearts."

Matthew 28:19b — Make disciples of all nations

1. Our imperative is "make disciples," surrounded by three participles.
2. The imperative, "make disciples," presents us with the challenge. Our goal is not simply to make converts or to solicit evangelistic decisions. Our goal is to work with people to produce whole-hearted, integrated, "obeying-all-things" disciples of Jesus.
3. The phrase *panta ta ethne* — "all ethnicities" — expands our mission beyond simply nations (i.e., geo-political entities that we see on our maps). The call identifies the discipling of all of the world's ethnic groups.

Make Disciples of All Nations: Three Life Lessons
- Lesson 1: A Mindset — living as a sent person
- Lesson 2: A Worldview — don't leave anyone out!
- Lesson 3: An Assurance — Jesus is always with us

Conclusion:
- As you are going, make disciples.
- Don't limit yourself to your own people, your own culture, or your own nation.
- Go with the accompanying power of God and assured presence of Jesus.

PAUL BORTHWICK (Lexington, MA)

Baptizing them in the name of the Father and of the Son and of the Holy Spirit
(Matthew 28:19c)

Introduction
Enthusiastic reflections

Why do we baptize people at Eastpoint?

- Thoughts and opinions, perceptions about baptism
- Strange Practices Illustration: Birthday Party
- Jesus thought baptism was important

> Then the eleven disciples went to Galilee, to the mountain where Jesus told them to go. When they saw him, they worshiped him; but some doubted. Then Jesus came to them and said, "All authority in heaven and on earth has been given to me. Therefore go and make disciples of all nations, baptizing them in the name of the Father and of the Son and of the Holy Spirit, and teaching them to obey everything I have commanded you. And surely I am with you always, to the very end of the age" (Matthew 28:16–20).

Reasons we baptize people at _____
- *Baptizo* — **Greek word for wash, soak, plunge, immerse, or dip**

History between OT and the time Jesus came

- Circumcision
- Passover
- The Law
- Sacrifice
- Ceremonial Cleansing
- Complete surrender to God, actually our God and the one true God
- Greek *baptizo*, or a Hebrew equivalent of *mikveh*, meaning to immerse in water

- Water is actually an important theme in Scripture
- Jesus takes something OLD and gives it NEW meaning

Some of the baptistries or *mikvehs* still hold water around or outside the temple.

Now listen to what the Apostle Paul writes.

> Or don't you know that all of us who were baptized into Christ Jesus were baptized into his death? We were therefore buried with him through baptism into death in order that, just as Christ was raised from the dead through the glory of the Father, we too may live a new life (Romans 6:3–4).

A real participation with Jesus

Jesus uses the physical participation of baptism to both symbolize and allow us to participate in His death, burial, and Resurrection, all of which He did for us in order to save us. In baptism you participate in all of it.

- Jesus was baptized
- John The Baptizer and Jesus

Matthew 3:11 — God's supernatural validation

> "I baptize you with water for repentance. But after me comes one who is more powerful than I, whose sandals I am not worthy to carry. He will baptize you with the Holy Spirit and fire."

Matthew 3:16 — it's the same spirit we receive

> As soon as Jesus was baptized, he went up out of the water. At that moment heaven was opened, and he saw the Spirit of God descending like a dove and alighting on him.

Acts 2:37–38

> When the people heard this, they were cut to the heart and said to Peter and the other apostles, "Brothers, what shall we do?"
>
> Peter replied, "Repent and be baptized, every one of you, in the name of Jesus Christ for the forgiveness of your sins. And you will receive the gift of the Holy Spirit."

So just to review:

1. Jesus submits to His Father's authority and is baptized by John, at which time God's Spirit comes down upon Jesus and He is divinely revealed as the Son of God.

2. Jesus fulfills the law. It is now through life lived in Jesus that the Jews and all people of the world will come to know the Father.

3. Jesus gives and sets the example of baptism for us to follow.
- Paul meets Jesus
- Story of Paul
- Paul's baptism

Acts 9:18–19 — Jesus' value of baptism

> Immediately, something like scales fell from Saul's eyes, and he could see again. He got up and was baptized, and after taking some food, he regained his strength.

The truth is, we don't want to be extremists who make baptism something it isn't, and we don't want to be minimalists teaching that it has little value or is optional.

One more thing about Paul

> Then he said: "The God of our ancestors has chosen you to know his will and to see the Righteous One

and to hear words from his mouth. You will be his witness to all people of what you have seen and heard. And now what are you waiting for? Get up, be baptized and wash your sins away, calling on his name" (Acts 22:14–16).

I don't know what you think after hearing all of this, seeing it for yourself in the life and ministry of Jesus, and in the life and ministry of His Apostles in the early church. It was the response of many people to the offer of salvation in the churches Paul planted, and here at EP as well. If after all of that you say, "I can see that Jesus wants me to be baptized, to participate in that very personal sacrifice of His death, burial and Resurrection for me, I want to honor Him, I want to be faithful to the request He asks of me," we can joyfully offer that to you. We can do it any time. But don't wait! This is for you if you know the Holy Spirit is speaking to you, or your heart is moved by the truth of Jesus.

SCOTT TAUBE (Portland, ME)

Teaching them to obey everything I have commanded you (Matthew 28:20a)

Illustration of needing to learn something that took training and practice.

Enthusiasm and Inspiration Are Not Enough

Imagine if our teachers relied too much on inspiration. What if your math teacher pumped you up telling you they believed in your ability to do multiplication?

"You've been created by God with a mind that is endowed with the power of mathematics! Multiplication is powerful! Useful! Life changing! Now go do multiplication!"

You might leave completely pumped to change the world through multiplication, but without knowledge and practice, you'll just bumble around in trial and error. We understand that we need to learn, practice, and grow in things such as school and sports. In the same way, the Scriptures teach us that God has given us leaders to equip "his people for works of service, so that the body of Christ may be built up until we all reach unity in the faith and in the knowledge of the Son of God and become mature, attaining to the whole measure of the fullness of Christ" (Ephesians 4:11–13). Jesus wants us to grow in maturity to our full potential as disciples.

1. Maturity doesn't occur overnight; it takes time and effort.
2. A pathway to maturity includes inspiration, education, and implementation.

As we dig deeper into the gospel of Jesus Christ, we see that God has a plan for our spiritual formation that is . . .

- Energized by supernatural power
- Rooted in Scripture (that's where we find the teachings of Jesus)
- Grounded in healthy practices
- Empowered through community

Whenever we start talking about supernatural power our ears perk up. When we hear about amazing things, we are often curious and a bit skeptical, yet many of us have experiences that we cannot explain because they are beyond human comprehension.

A. Positive Supernatural Power Comes through Faith

1. Faith is not merely intellectual.
2. Trust is an essential element of faith.
3. Trust is a key factor in relational obedience.

Illustration of the connection of trust and obedience

B. Trusting and becoming a Christian

As we come to know Christ Jesus we begin to trust Him and His teaching. Eventually we come to believe that He is the Messiah, the son of the living God, and we are faced with an important faith decision. Will we act on this belief? Will we commit to proclaim Jesus as Lord and be baptized as a sign of that committed relationship? Just like a ring is a sign of a marriage commitment, so baptism is a sign of our commitment with Jesus.

C. The Supernatural Gift of the Holy Spirit

Additionally, we are promised a supernatural, relational gift . . .

> "Repent and be baptized, every one of you, in the name of Jesus Christ for the forgiveness of your sins. And you will receive the gift of the Holy Spirit" (Acts 2:38).

The Holy Spirit binds himself to us and helps us to follow Jesus, remember and obey His teachings, encourages us in times of trouble, comforts us in distress, gives us courage in the face of adversity, gifts us to do the work of God, intercedes for us before God, and transforms our very character to become more like Jesus. How can we live in Christ without the Holy Spirit? The Spirit is influencing us right at this moment to have faith and act in accordance with God's will. You probably feel his presence moving you to align with God in worship, prayer, and to walk in faithful obedience.

Introductory Question: How do we know that the inside voice we hear, or the gut feeling we have, is the Holy Spirit? How do we test that out?

A. The Holy Spirit Is Always Moving Us Toward Alignment with Scripture.

1. Obedience to Scripture is a vital aspect of discipleship, but it must always be superseded by a love for God and others (John 13:34–35; 1 Corinthians 13:1–4).

2. Our growth as disciples of Jesus must be approached as a relational opportunity rather than a dogmatic enterprise. Consequently, a love for God and others must flow through every aspect of our spiritual teaching and practices.

Illustration from the Road to Emmaus

When the resurrected Jesus spent time with disciples on the road to Emmaus they asked each other, "Were not our hearts burning within us while he talked with us on the road and opened the Scriptures to us?" (Luke 24:32).

They were so excited about their experience, that they traveled through the night to share with others what had happened. This is a beautiful illustration of the type of motivation that is at the core of our spiritual development.

B. Christ's Master Plan

Furthermore, Jesus commissions us to make disciples; His followers model this for us, and then urge us to become diligent in continuing this process. The Gospel of Matthew closes with Jesus commissioning his apostles stating:

> "All authority in heaven and on earth has been given to me. Therefore go and make disciples of all nations, baptizing them in the name of the Father and of the Son and of the Holy Spirit, and teaching them to obey everything I have commanded you. And surely I am with you always, to the very end of the age" (Matthew 28:18–20).

Here, the disciples receive a basic template for spiritual development beginning with hearing the gospel, progressing to commitment and baptism, then continuing with instruction and obedience. It should be noted that people are discipled to conversion, not simply after conversion. This is well illustrated in Jesus' ministry (John 1–2; Luke 5:1–11); we see through the gospels that the disciples were following Jesus and listening to Him some time before they placed their faith in Him. Consequently, spiritual formation begins before conversion and continues afterward.

In the first chapters of the Book of Acts we see this process modeled by the Apostles and early disciples as they devote themselves to the core practices of teaching, community, prayer, generosity, hospitality, and evangelism (Acts 2:42–47). Luke repeatedly emphasizes these elements and reveals a fruitful progression of healthy spiritual formation in both the church at large and in the lives of individuals. The church grows in numbers and in leadership. Men like Barnabas and Philip are the products of a discipleship process that they pass on as they are sent to plant new congregations.

Inspirational Note:

Here's an amazing thought — You are the new generation of Christians and all of you are an integral part of God's Kingdom plan!

> In order to "learn God" and cultivate intimacy with God, human persons need guidance and a guide. The need for guidance is the reason Christian spiritual teachers have, for centuries, nurtured and cultivated practices of spiritual direction and formation. — Kay Northcutt[1]

A. The Principle of Teaching and Imitation

1. Listen, watch, learn, and do
2. Scripture directs us in how to listen, watch, learn, and do.

---

1. Kay Northcutt, *Kindling Desire for God: Preaching as Spiritual Direction* (Minneapolis, MN: Fortress Press, 2009), Kindle 208.

B. Discerning the Voice of God through Scripture

1. Be careful to whom you are listening

In a world of competing influences, it is important to prioritize sources of information because they do not speak to us with the same authority. The Wesleyan Quadrilateral is very helpful when weighing the influence of different sources when considering how we view issues and practice our faith as Christ followers. Before adopting influence and practices, it is wise to evaluate them, giving the most authority to Scripture, second to tradition, third to reason, and last to experience.

2. American culture is upside down

C. God Uses Our Distinctiveness to Glorify Himself and Draw Others to Him.

1. Christian obedience is distinctive — sometimes honored, sometimes persecuted.
2. Areas of distinctiveness.

Illustrations of Distinctiveness

D. The Goal of Obedience is Character Transformation

Those who choose to follow Jesus are a new creation, and it is amazing how young adults in our congregation come out of a worldly view of sexual relations and adopt the values of Jesus. These are producing amazing fruit in healthy friendships that develop into committed and faithful relationships. By demonstrating that we can be faithful to God in sexuality before marriage, we establish a firm foundation of fidelity within marriage. God has a purpose for purity that develops character in profound ways.

Challenge: BE DISTINCTIVE! BE SALT AND LIGHT!

A. Example of Jesus and His Disciples

    1. The 12 Apostles
    2. The Early Church in Acts

    Day after day, in the temple courts and from house to house, they never stopped teaching and proclaiming the good news that Jesus is the Messiah (Acts 5:42).

B. The Church Has a "Family-Style" Model for Personal Growth

    1. How people grow in maturity

I can honestly say that this is how I learned 99% of Jesus' teachings. I learned to pray by listening to others pray and imitating them. I learned to read and understand the Scriptures by watching other Christians do this in a small group. I learned to be generous, compassionate, discerning, and caring while in the presence of devoted followers of Jesus. Although I sometimes gleaned information from books, articles, and videos, I learned to practice faith in Jesus by watching others.

Illustration of awkwardness and growth

C. Importance of Small Groups

We have great groups within the church. Some people hang back from joining a group because of fear of awkwardness and embarrassment, but I want to urge you not to be afraid. We are all simply striving to follow Jesus and help each other along the way. Even as a more seasoned Christian I learn lessons from new disciples, and I am reminded that sincere love of God and others is the goal of our faith. After following Jesus for over 30 years, it is still exciting to hear faith stories from young Christians who are filled with enthusiasm and the grace of God.

Invitation

Summary Statements

The stakes are high; God is calling this generation to "live up to what we have already attained." (Philippians 3:16). We have been given an unparalleled set of resources with more access to information than at any other time in history. Christ has passed the torch of faith to us, and it is our responsibility, with the help of the Holy Spirit to enliven the souls of today.

I want to encourage you to step into a relational obedience that builds character through grace . . . an obedience that is energized by supernatural power, rooted in the Scriptures, grounded in healthy practices, and empowered through community.

- Perhaps today is the day you commit to following Jesus and step into obedience. I want to invite you to celebrate that through baptism even this very day.
- Maybe you've slipped into some unhealthy practices. Make a decision to repent, get back on track, and engage in a group.

- If you're a seasoned disciple, the Lord needs you to help teach and train His people to obey. Jesus has poured the richness of His grace into you. It's time to rise and become a servant-leader. You don't need to know everything, just pass along what Jesus has commanded you. And here's the promise — Jesus WILL be with us until the very end!

LARRY STRONDAK (Westbrook, ME)

And surely I am with you always
(Matthew 28:20b)

Introduction

- "Make disciples of all nations?" — How can we get there?
- Illustration: Without Him, we can do nothing!
- Between the greatest historical event and the greatest commission was the greatest proclamation: "All authority in heaven and on earth has been given to me" (Matthew 28:18).
- The greatest commission ended with the greatest promise: "And surely I am with you always" (Matthew 28:20).

I. "God is with us" — the greatest partnership

A. Our most powerful partner (illustration: from rejecter to disciple)

B. Our most loving and caring partner (illustration: He touched the lepers)

C. Our most faithful and ready partner (illustration: He restored our faith)

II. "God is with us" — the greatest relationship

A. We have a lasting relationship with Jesus

B. We have a faithful relationship with Jesus

C. We have a loving relationship with Jesus

III. "God is with us" — the greatest blessing

    A. Turn our focus back to Jesus
       (Illustration: the police raid in China)

    B. Turn our fears into joy

    C. "God with us" becomes "God in us"

    D. Therefore as you go make disciples

WING WONG (Manchester, NH)

To the very end of the age
(Matthew 28:20c)

Main idea: The last seven words of Jesus in the Gospel of Matthew are about commitment, and the question is, How committed are you?

Introduction:

- The Red-Circled Day — Story about a day circled on the calendar. The red-circled day always seemed so far away. Temptation would be to race through the days to get to the red-circled day. However, the call on our lives is to make the most of every day.
- Commitment — The last seven words of Jesus are about commitment.
- How committed are you? — Story about family fair. Daughters tried to get me to shave my head. They asked, "How committed are you to this?" This is the question for today. How committed are we to being disciples and making disciples?

Four Lessons about Commitment:

1. Commitment Is Not a Problem for Jesus

Babe Ruth Story — pointed to center field. Jesus pointed to an empty tomb. He kept His promise. He can be trusted.

> He is committed to empower us — all authority is His.
> He is committed to be with us always.

2. Commitment Determines Direction

To be a disciple means to be a person whose commitment to Jesus determines their direction.

> Story of Ruth's commitment to Naomi
> Story of Elijah in 1 Kings 17 – "So he did . . ."

3. Commitment Always Overrules Comfort

Jesus rarely chose the comfortable route.

> No Trespassing, Keep Out! — Story of sign on bedroom door. Often how we treat the Lord. But He is looking for an all-access pass to our lives.

> Story of Peter and Cornelius in Acts 10 — willing to get uncomfortable for the gospel. Are you ready to allow commitment to overrule comfort?

4. Commitment Invites the Power of God

We are not empty handed — Story about Joe the rancher. He gave me everything I needed to complete the mission. The Lord gives us the best gift — the Holy Spirit.

> The power of God comes through radical obedience — 2 Chronicles 16:9

Conclusion: How committed are you?

- Story of Simen Krueger — Cross country skier who never gave up.
- Jesus has drawn a red circle around the day of His return. Until then, let's make the most of our time by passionately and boldly sharing Jesus with others.

BRIAN MOWREY (Bethel, CT)

The Priority of Discipleship
(Matthew 28:16–20)

Subject: What did Jesus instruct His disciples to do after He told them to meet Him in Galilee following His Resurrection?

Complement: Though some of them doubted, they have His authority to make disciples of all peoples and they are to teach them and to baptize them in the name of the Father, Son, and Holy Spirit. Jesus would be with them always as they carry out this command.

Idea: Jesus instructed His disciples after He told them to meet Him in Galilee following His Resurrection. Even though some of them doubted, they had His authority to go and make disciples of all peoples and that they are to teach them and to baptize them in the name of the Father, Son, and Holy Spirit and that Jesus would be with them always as they carry out this command.

Homiletical Idea: There's no doubt about it, discipleship matters when it comes to Jesus building the church.

Purpose: As a result of hearing this sermon, I want my listeners to understand the priority of discipleship.

Introduction

I. We sometimes think that evangelism is all there is.

A. This text is often used as an evangelism or "missions" text.

B. I was involved in campus ministry while in college that focuses on evangelism.

C. We may think that this biblical text is about going, missions, and evangelizing.

D. We sometimes think that evangelizing is all there is.

(But . . .)

II. Going is the route and discipleship is the goal.

A. "Make disciples" is the primary emphasis.

B. I got an understanding about the power of discipleship when I was a pastor.

C. We may find it difficult to get our brains wrapped around what I'm talking about.

D. Going is the route and discipleship is the goal.

(This text isn't mainly about going or evangelism, but about discipleship.)

III. There's no doubt about it, discipleship matters when it comes to growing the church.

A. The text says that some disciples of Jesus worshiped, but some doubted.

B. Being a disciple, a learner of Jesus, is the road toward maturity.

C. Maturity doesn't come easily.

Conclusion

There's no doubt about it, discipleship matters when it comes to growing the church.

SCOTT GIBSON (South Hamilton, MA, and Waco, TX)

Appendix 2

Life Group Study Guide
The Call of Discipleship

Jamie Lankford (Warwick, RI)

Small Group Discussion

Big Idea: Jesus' call to discipleship is for everyone.

Small Group Tip: Don't be afraid of silence when leading a small group. Always allow time for people to think about and formulate a response to a question. Remember that a leader's transparency and vulnerability can make a big difference in how those in a small group interact and respond.

Icebreaker: (We recommend beginning each small group session with a question or exercise that starts a discussion to put people at ease with sharing more.) What is the most exciting phone call you have ever received?

Who has had the greatest influence or impact on you as it relates to your relationship with God? What did they do?

Read Matthew 28:16–20 (Find a volunteer in your group to read aloud).

When Jesus speaks in this text, what are the action words that stand out to you? What does each one mean to you?

Jesus' Example: Consider each of the passages in Matthew of Jesus' examples of how to make disciples, and answer the questions that follow.

Read Matthew 4:18–22.

What does Jesus do in this passage?

What example does this set for us?

What relationships do you have where you could invite someone into a disciple-making relationship?

Read Matthew 9:9–13.

What are the different parties involved in this story?

Which of the parties do you relate to the most and why?

What relationships do you currently have that would be similar to Matthew and the friends he invited to celebrate with him?

Read Matthew 10.

What would your response be if Jesus sent you out like He did the 12 in this passage?

What would this look like in your everyday life right now?

Discipleship Action Step: (Each week the group will be challenged to put what they are learning into practice through some sort of action item. Be sure to follow up in your next group session to allow people to share their experience and what they learned through it.) This week, spend time praying that God will open up opportunities for you to share your story with someone who doesn't know Him. Perhaps a first step while you are doing this would be to write your faith story and share it with someone in your group.

At The Mountain

Small Group Discussion

Big Idea: Becoming a disciple means we learn to trust Jesus.

Icebreaker: When was the last time you tried something new? What was that experience like?

Why is trust important in a relationship?

Read Matthew 28:16–20.

When was the last time you did something you believed Jesus was asking you to do, and what did you do?

When you do not put your trust in Jesus, who or what do you put your trust in?

Picture yourself on this mountain at this moment. What would your response be to Jesus? Why would you respond that way? Have you responded to this call?

Read Romans 8:35–39.

What things stand out to you in this passage?

Combine this passage with the commission Jesus gives on the mountain. What impact does this have on you when it comes to obeying his call?

Discipleship Action Step: Read through Matthew 28:16–20. Reflect on each part of this call. Which part or parts are the most challenging for you? Ask God to give you boldness and His strength as you seek to obey His commission.

They Worshiped Him

Small Group Discussion

Big Idea: Discipleship starts with worship.

Icebreaker: What is your favorite sports team? What is your favorite sports moment?

Do you remember the first time you encountered Jesus? What was your response?

Read Matthew 28:16–20.

Before you heard this message, how did you view/define worship?

What is your understanding of worship now?

Read Romans 12:1.

What does it look like in your everyday life to "offer your body as a living sacrifice?"

Read Isaiah 1:2–15.

Why do you think God found Israel's expressions of "worship" unacceptable?

When does "worship" simply become ritual?

Where have you allowed worship to become ritual in your life?

How can we get to the place in our lives where we are worshiping God with all we are and all we do?

Discipleship Action Step: What is one practical thing you will do this week that will reflect true and proper worship of God? Be prepared to come back next week to share how you did this.

But Some Doubted

Small Group Discussion

Big Idea: Faith and doubt are not in opposition; they are in constant companionship.

Icebreaker: When is the last time you had one of those "it's too good to be true" moments?

What/who do you have the most difficulty trusting?

When is doubt good?

Read Matthew 28:16–20 (focus is 17b).

Why do you think some of his followers doubted?

Read Matthew 14: 22–33.

In this story, you can see the close relationship between faith and doubt in what Peter did. What demonstrated Peter's faith? What demonstrated Peter's doubt?

Right now, which action of Peter do you most relate to (getting out of the boat or taking eyes off Jesus) and why?

Respond to this statement: Our great doubt is not so much in the existence of God, but we doubt whether or not God is good.

Do you agree with this? Why or why not?

Has there been a time you have doubted the goodness of God?

What is the difference between faith and certainty?

What are some doubts about God that are currently keeping you from fully trusting Him?

What is the role a small group should play in our lives as we wrestle with doubt?

Discipleship Action Step: Spend time this week making a list of doubts you have about God. Devote time each day confessing these to God. Share your experience with someone from your small group.

All Authority in Heaven and on Earth Has Been Given to Me

Small Group Discussion

Big Idea: It's only through the authority of Jesus
that disciples are made.

Icebreaker: What do you think of when you hear the word authority?

Read Matthew 28:16–20.

Identify the uses of the word "all" in the text.

What is the significance of Jesus having all authority? What does this mean?

What impact does the fact that Jesus has been given all authority have on us as we become disciples of Him?

Knowing Jesus has been given all authority, how does this impact your response to His call to make disciples?

The authority of Jesus is specifically for the purpose of making disciples. This authority is all we need to make disciples. Why is it so important we understand this?

How have you seen the authority of Jesus in your life? In the lives of others?

Where do you struggle the most in seeing the authority (power) of Jesus in your life?

Discipleship Action Step: Read through the first seven (7) chapters in Acts (one per day). Note every time the authority of Jesus shows up in the lives of His followers. Reflect on how this same authority also resides in you.

Therefore Go

Small Group Discussion

Big Idea: The power to accomplish our mission
comes only from Jesus.

Icebreaker: When was the last time you had no power in your home? How long was it out?

What does it mean to be a disciple of Jesus?

Read Matthew 28:16–20.

What does Jesus mean when He says, "therefore as you go"?

What does "going" look like for you?

If true discipleship means following Jesus, what does it mean to follow Him?

Read John 15:1–8

What does abiding in Jesus mean? How do we do this on a daily basis?

What prevents you from abiding in Jesus?

What is the fruit Jesus is talking about? How is this reflected in your life?

How does abiding in Jesus connect with the mission of going?

Disciple Action Step: Reflect some more on John 15. Spend time this week abiding in Jesus. Over the remainder of this study continue to do this and see what fruit it produces. Share with your group what you are doing to abide.

Make Disciples of All Nations

Small Group Discussion

Big Idea: Don't limit disciple making to your own people, culture, or nation.

Icebreaker: If you could travel anywhere, where would you go and why?

How would you define the term "nations"?

Read Matthew 28:16–20.

Compare this to similar passages in Mark 16:15–18; Luke 24:45–49; Acts 1:9, and John 20:21–22.

What are some similarities in each of these passages?

What are some differences?

Jesus tells us we are to make disciples of all nations. Why is this so important?

Not everyone can travel to other countries. How do you carry out this part of Jesus' mission where you currently live, work, and play?

How do you live everyday of your life as someone who is sent?

At work —

In your neighborhood —

At school —

Why is it difficult to reach out to people who are different from us? Who are the most difficult people for you to reach out to?

Discipleship Action Step: If you don't already know this, do some research about the city you live in. Find out how many different ethnicities, nations, and cultures are represented in your city. What can you do to reach out to some of them?

Baptizing Them

Small Group Discussion

Big Idea: Baptism is a key part of the discipleship process.

Icebreaker: What is the most moving thing you have ever witnessed?

Before hearing this message, what was your understanding of baptism?

Read Matthew 28:16–20.

The Greek word for baptism here is *baptizo* which means to wash, soak, plunge, immerse, or dip. How does that impact your understanding about baptism?

Read the following passages: Romans 6:3–4; Matthew 3:16–17; Acts 2:37–38, 9:18–19.

Knowing Jesus was Himself baptized, how does this affect how you view baptism?

What do you notice about the place of baptism in each of these passages?

Why is baptism important and part of the discipleship process?

If you have been baptized, why did you make that decision?

If you haven't been baptized, what is holding you back?

Discipleship Action Step: If you have not yet taken the step of being baptized, consider taking that next step.

Teaching Them to Obey Everything I Have Commanded You

Small Group Discussion

Big Idea: Obedience is essential to discipleship.

Icebreaker: Who greatly inspires you? Why?

How do you tend to learn the best?

Read Matthew 28:16–20.

What has been your experience with teaching others? How have you learned what you now know?

What is your understanding of the role of the Holy Spirit in the disciple-making process?

How do we know we are hearing the Holy Spirit?

In what kind of environment do you tend to grow the most spiritually?

What does your role as someone who teaches people to obey all of Jesus' teachings look like today?

Discipleship Action Step: Who is it in your life that you can begin to show the ways of Jesus? Pray for opportunities to share this with them.

And Surely I Am With You Always

Small Group Discussion

Big Idea: We are never alone; God is always with us.

Icebreaker: If you could go on a long trip with anyone (other than a family member) who would it be and why?

Has there ever been a time in your life where you have felt completely alone?

What or who do you tend to turn to when things become difficult or you face significant challenges in your life?

Read Matthew 28:16-20.

When you hear the words "and surely I am with you always," what does this mean to you?

Share a time when you have experienced Jesus being with you.

When it comes to following Jesus, what are the parts of your life that are the most difficult to follow Him? Why?

How are you at sharing your story of what God has done for you with someone else? If this is difficult for you, why is it difficult?

Why is it crucial for us to realize that Jesus is with us always, especially as we are making disciples?

Discipleship Action Step: Spend time this week thanking Jesus for being with us always. Take some time and reflect on those situations you thought were impossible in your life. In those seasons or circumstances, did you recognize that Jesus was with you? If not, how might that circumstance have been different?

To The Very End of the Age

Small Group Discussion

Big Idea: We are to be unwaveringly committed
to His call on our lives to make disciples.

Icebreaker: When was the last time you failed to keep a commitment? Read Matthew 28:16–20.

What does "to the very end of the age" mean?

How does this pertain to you as a follower of Jesus?

How does the life of Jesus reflect His commitment to us? What should our response to Him be?

Commitment determines direction. Who or what are you currently committed to and in what direction is this leading you? How does our commitment to Jesus impact our direction?

Why do we default into what is comfortable? How does this impact our ability to follow Jesus? How does this impact disciple making?

Do you have a difficult time recognizing the power of God in your life? Why or why not? When have you experienced God's power in your life?

What keeps you from depending on God?

Discipleship Action Step: This week ask yourself, "How committed am I to following Jesus?" What needs to change? Where have you become "comfortable"?

Growing the Church: The Priority of Discipleship

Small Group Discussion

Big Idea: Going is the route and discipleship is
the goal.

Icebreaker: If you could spend time doing anything you wanted, what would you do?

Has there ever been a time when someone told you something and you entirely missed their point?

When you hear the passage this series is based on, what immediately comes to mind?

Read Matthew 28:16–20 (maybe someone can recite it from memory). What does it mean to be a disciple?

If you think you have been discipled, what has that looked like for you? Who or what has had the greatest impact on you?

What is your role in being a disciple of Jesus? In other words, how much of the responsibility of being a disciple of Jesus is yours?

Why do we sometimes resist growth in our faith?

Where would you say you are right now as a disciple of Jesus — heading backward, stuck/stagnant, growing? Why?

Discipleship Action Step: What are your next steps in growing as a disciple of Jesus? Take some time and write these down. Pray for God to direct each step. Seek out someone who will walk with you through these.

Appendix 3

Personal Growth Assessment

Peter Balantine (Newburyport, MA)

Directions

a. Respond to each statement according to the following scale:

0 — Not at all, never
1 — Some of the time, once in a while
2 — Most of the time, usually true
3 — Consistently, definitely true

b. Using the scoring sheet, write your response to each statement in the block whose number corresponds to that number question.

c. Important: Answer according to who you are, not who you would like to be or think you ought to be. How true are these statements of you? What has been your experience? To what degree do these statements reflect your usual tendencies?

1. I believe God is both holy and ruler over all His creation, and He loves and cares for me personally. **0 1 2 3**

2. I believe human beings are broken because of sin. Our sin separates us from God for eternity. **0 1 2 3**

3. I believe Jesus Christ died on the Cross for me, paying the penalty for my sin, so that I could be restored to a right relationship with God. **0 1 2 3**

4. On my own, and with others, I regularly praise God for who He is and what He has done. **0 1 2 3**

5. I regularly take time out from work to rest. **0 1 2 3**

6. I explain to others what God has done in my life through Jesus. **0 1 2 3**

7. I trust God rather than relying on my own ability to control my life. **0 1 2 3**

8. I have a confident assurance for the future based on God's character and power. I have an inner contentment despite my circumstances. **0 1 2 3**

9. I do not give up when I am afraid, but instead rely on God's strength. **0 1 2 3**

10. I believe all those who put their trust in Jesus are a part of God's family — regardless of age, race, income level, or nationality. None of us is alone. **0 1 2 3**

11. I believe each of us is an important part of the body of Christ. I need others and others need me. **0 1 2 3**

12. I am committed to a particular group of people who care for each other and spur one another on in following Christ. This is a group that knows me, prays for me, and helps me to be accountable for how I live my life. **0 1 2 3**

13. I really listen to people when they talk to me and I consistently speak truthfully to others. **0 1 2 3**

14. I speak directly with people I am in conflict with and seek to forgive and be forgiven. **0 1 2 3**

15. I am thoughtful, considerate, and kind as I deal with others. **0 1 2 3**

16. I consistently work toward maintaining peace with others, avoiding inciteful words and actions. **0 1 2 3**

17. I bear with others, keeping my composure even when people or circumstances irritate me. **0 1 2 3**

18. I believe I can live by God's power against sin. **0 1 2 3**

19. I believe the Holy Spirit lives inside me and helps me become holy as well as empowers me for service. **0 1 2 3**

20. I believe that I have authority in spiritual conflict through Christ. **0 1 2 3**

21. I read, study, memorize, and meditate on the Scriptures to know God, gain truth, and find direction for my life. **0 1 2 3**

22. I periodically abstain from food, drink, media, and consumption in general in order to maintain control over my wants and desires. **0 1 2 3**

23. I regularly confess my sins to God and others. **0 1 2 3**

24. I have the capacity and strength to say no to my appetites and desires. **0 1 2 3**

25. I make good decisions for my life based on godly principles. **0 1 2 3**

26. I am a truthful and authentic person. Who I am on the outside matches who I am on the inside. **0 1 2 3**

27. I believe I am to put Christ first in all areas of my life, including my time, my resources, and my daily activities. **0 1 2 3**

28. I believe God cares for the hungry, the sick, the prisoner, the stranger, and the broken-hearted. **0 1 2 3**

29. I know and use the spiritual gifts God has given me. This applies both within the Christian community and in my daily work. **0 1 2 3**

30. I pray regularly for God's Kingdom to come to this earth, recognizing that prayer is a vital work of the ministry. **0 1 2 3**

31. I give away my money and resources to fulfill God's purposes. **0 1 2 3**

32. I am comfortable with who I am and who I am not. I do not underestimate or exaggerate my strengths and weaknesses. **0 1 2 3**

33. I seek the welfare of those who suffer or are treated unfairly. **0 1 2 3**

34. I show sacrificial and unconditional love for others. **0 1 2 3**

Personal Growth Assessment Scoring Sheet

Beliefs

1. __ Personal God
18. __ Living by God's Power
2. __ Sin and Brokenness
19. __ Holy Spirit
3. __ Christ's Work

10. __ Unity
27. __ Kingdom Priorities
11. __ Diversity
28. __Compassion
20. __Spiritual Warfare

Habits

4. __ Worship
21. __ God's Word
5. __ Rest
22. __ Fasting
6. __ Sharing the Gospel
23. __ Confession

12. __ Small Group
29. __ Spiritual Gifts
13. __ Listening/Talking
30. __Intercession
14. __ Resolving Conflict
31. __Giving

Character Qualities

7. __ Faith
24. __ Self Control
8. __ Hope
25. __ Wisdom
9. __ Courage
26. __ Integrity

15. __ Gentleness
32. __ Humility
16. __ Peace
33. __ Justice
17. __ Patience
34. __ Love

(__)   (__)   (__)   (__)
GRACE   **COMMUNITY**   **HOLINESS**   **SERVICE**

PETER BALENTINE (Newburyport, MA)